The Essential Guide to Marketing Your ADR Practice

Tools to Thrive ~ Not Just Survive

Natalie J. Armstrong

Powered by Golden Media Publishing
www.MarketingADR.com

The Essential Guide to Marketing Your ADR Practice for the ADR Industry

A practice-building primer for Mediators, Arbitrators, and Peacemakers

COPYRIGHT © 2001 Golden Media

ISBN : 0-9723419-0-0

Printed in the USA 2001

Published by Golden Media Publishing in Los Angeles, California.

The Essential Guide To Marketing Your ADR Practice

TABLE OF CONTENTS

ACKNOWLEDGMENTS

I can't begin to imagine how this book would have come about without the assistance and support of my family, friends, and clients.

I was lucky enough to have been born into a family that is more than just a big family – we could overthrow small countries. Every sense of communication has been directly derived from countless Sunday dinners and holiday feasts. Just getting through a meal in such a large family required the use of debate, humor and hyjincks to a level that the Barnum and Bailey Circus would appreciate.

However, it is my parents to whom I owe the most. They are the standard to which I always attempt to rise. They were and remain incomparable teachers and friends who gave me my love for education, taught me to follow where curiosity leads, never be afraid of an adventure, and provide me still with a sense of rootedness and confidence. While I was growing up I can't remember how many times my mother reminded me that if I didn't like something I should change it (she is quite confident that there are very few things that humans can't change). She embodies the strength of a saint (probably due to having to put up with all of us) and the grace and peace of a woman who has known great sorrow and even more delight. The depth of her constantly surprises me. (She also taught me how to play hooky and get away with it).

As for my father, he used to wear a tee-shirt that read "No man is truly worthless, he can always serve as a bad example". This tee-shirt was given to him in jest – since there are few folks who serve as such an ideal example. He also instilled in me the idea that communication is the key that will unlock countless barriers and enhance even more opportunities. It is from him that I get my love of ADR and all its potential. As a gentleman rancher he trained me to rely on my knowledge of myself more than the opinions of others, to trust everyone but always cut the cards (from his own hero – J.F.K.), how to drive fast enough to beat the local boys at their own race, and that you're never too old to be a daddy's girl.

My kid sister (she hates when I call her that) has been my partner in crime, my travel companion, my great and dear friend and more often than she'll admit to – she's been my hero. She taught me the power of treating my family like guests and my guests like family. Her humanity is incomparable.

Elizabeth, my young daughter, is whom I want to be when I grow up. She has no concept of limits only of her own infinite potential. She has shown me who I am in the mirrors of her eyes and kept the world in simplistic perspective for me. She never holds a grudge, always laughs with her whole heart and body, doesn't begrudge anyone, anywhere, ever, the chance to be heard and appreciated, and to say please and thank you, and eat whatever the hostess serves.

And last but by no means least I'd like to thank my mate, Drew. He is my partner, my best friend, my confident, my beacon, my straight-man in this comedy we call living and the love of my life. He never holds against me my penchant for ice-cream in the dead of night and warms my feet after my nocturnal visit to the freezer. He keeps me constantly laughing – frequently about myself - and always lends his shoulders for support, for hard work, and very often for me to climb upon for a better view. His happy and loving influence is in everything I do and am. Without his gentle prodding, cajoling, and encouraging this book would not be in your hands.

In concert they gave me my love for communication, laughter and life and continue to do so daily.

I must also thank those friends who have directly contributed to the making of this book. Valerie Valdez for her patient editing of what must have originally looked like the random placement of nouns, verbs, adverbs and adjectives by someone who had never experienced the English language. And to Todd and Mo Bingham who have proven through their own successes that it could be done – then helped me do it. I am in their debt.

To my clients and colleagues – thank you. Thank you for your continued support, enthusiasm, and passion for the industry I love and believe in heart and soul.

Natalie J. Armstrong
August, 2001

Introduction

▾ ▾ ▾

Experience has taught me that there is one chief reason why some people succeed and others fail. The difference is not one of knowing, but of doing. The successful man is not so superior in ability as in action. So far as success can be reduced to a formula, it consists of this: doing what you know you should do."

Roger Babson,
the man who called the 1929 market crash
and made enough money to start Babson College.

In a free association game with service providers the most common response to the word "marketing" was "advertising". The most common response to "advertising" was "sales" and the most common response to "sales" was "car salesmen" and "telemarketing". When we then asked them how they felt about these two responses they let us know that they associated marketing with the "slick" maneuvering of car salesmen and the untimely and interruptive abilities of telemarketers. In sum, two professions they would never aspire to be a part of.

In short that they were uncomfortable with the task of marketing their practices and more importantly they thought that their prospective clients would view them as equals to the "slick" salesmen they themselves didn't like. Practitioners told us they were quite comfortable with what they were doing in their own Alternative Dispute Resolution (ADR) practice, law firm or career of choice that had segued into an ADR practice, but that they had no education or experience with marketing. They didn't received their ADR education new business would find it's way to them.

THIS METHOD OF MARKETING DOES NOT WORK

It especially does not work for arbitrators and mediators. As arbitrators and mediators we are concerned with maintaining our neutrality and surpassing the codes of conduct and rules of ethics we impose upon ourselves. We expect ourselves and others in our industry to conduct themselves with the highest possible standards of human conduct. We are after all professional negotiators, facilitators, communicators, listeners, and peacemakers.

As folks who pride themselves on providing solutions not problems, comfort not discontent, and hope not dismay, how can we promote and market ourselves without violating the expected standards of conduct for our industry and violating the trust of potential clients?

SO WHAT DOES WORK?

What is the magic bullet that will propel your practice into success? Most marketing experts will tell you that there is no magic bullet, they tell you instead that marketing is a complex, difficult, many-layered task that requires years of experience and education. Well... as it turns out, I happen to think they're wrong.

THERE IS A MAGIC BULLET

A magic bullet that anyone with any amount of education or experience can employ for success. A magic bullet that is so simple and so obvious that most of you reading this book won't believe it until you've tried it. And if you've already tried it then you know I'm right.

So what is the ultimate marketing tool, the perfect answer to all questions, the definitive technique for transforming your practice?

Well, before I answer that, let's go back a bit. When I was a little girl my father once told me that no man is completely worthless. He can always serve as a bad example. Well that's what the typical car salesman and telemarketer can do for you (my apologies to all the car salesmen and telemarketers who have done a very fine job at their chosen profession – and there are many of you).

The important question here is why. What is it about their techniques we're uncomfortable with? Why do we bristle at their strategies to get us to buy? Why do we view marketing with such trepidation (we're professional communicators for goodness sake)? So what can they teach us?

Let's start with auto sales. Think about how you feel when you're engaged in a conversation with a salesman on a car lot. Do you feel comfortable with your automotive knowledge? Are you confident that you will be able to negotiate the best possible deal for yourself? Though there are a few people who actually enjoy negotiating for and purchasing their cars most of us do not. More often we feel at a disadvantage because we lack the technical auto information the salesman seems so easily to spew forth and we're being put in a spot to trust the very person whom we hold suspect to owning all kinds of undesirable attributes. We frequently feel like we're not in control of the buying process. We feel like we're being played and manipulated for someone else's enjoyment and profit. Something we certainly don't want our potential clients to feel.

And how about the telemarketer? Why do we view telemarketing as such a loathsome practice? No matter where he's calling from or on which topic he can always find the time in our day when are the most occupied and attempt to sell us product that we would never use. We regard his nerve and audacity with disgust. Many of us reply with negative words that equal the heat of a supernova. Others of us just drop the phone back into its cradle and go on with our task at hand. The last thing in the world we want from out prospects is that kind of response.

Just as one bad experience with a car salesman or telemarketer imbues their entire industry with self-serving interests that we find so offensive, one poor experience of a disputant with an ADR provider will imbue our whole profession with mistrust.

So how do we avoid being viewed as we view them?

Read on.

The 4 Ps (& More)

You frequently hear about the four Ps in marketing. Traditionally they are Product, Price, Place, and Promotion. However, these "Ps" are just the beginning. For any service provider who's serious about their marketing there are a few more "Ps" (in fact, we think there should be 15 "Ps"). They follow.

PRODUCT

For our purposes, product should be read as "service." Product (or service) is what you sell. For ADR professionals, this may be just one process along the spectrum of dispute resolution services or many. Frequently, when providers offer potential clients a vast array of processes up front, the consumer is overwhelmed with options they may or may not understand. If you offer more than one service, consider educating your consumer about each process, or offer them a "customized" process that is created on a customer-by-customer basis. You must also consider that you're not just selling a process.

Remember to take into consideration those intangible Products you are selling (e.g. hope, solutions, resolution, peace of mind, etc.).

PLACE

Conrad Hilton's belief that success has to do with three things: location, location, location, does not necessarily apply to our industry. If your practice is designed for clients to come to you, then of course location is very important. Providing a convenient location (think about available parking as well as amenities like restaurants, and so on.) may be key in attracting clients. On the other hand, if your practice "delivers" its service to clients, then location can be a secondary concern.

PRICE

This "P" is a particularly sticky wicket in the ADR industry. With so many providers offering their services at no charge, and numerous private and public organizations requesting, if not demanding, that services be provided on a voluntary basis, many of us are stuck about how to price our services. In some geographic, demographic and psychographic markets, there remains an argument about whether non-attorney practitioners should be paid the same as attorney practitioners. What it all boils down to is this: First, choose which of four categories your practice falls into: voluntary, for pay, mostly voluntary with some pay, or mostly for pay with some voluntary.

If your practice is of the volunteer variety and you like it that way, then you have no pricing issues, only of finding enough community and court panels for volunteers.

If your practice is primary volunteer with some for pay cases and you want to move it into the paying category as the primary portion of your practice, there are solutions. To make a transition from a primary-volunteer practice into paying cases you should be careful to volunteer within groups who will provide you either referrals to paying cases or who, as repeat clients, will pay for future services. Another avenue of transition lies in your calendar. Allow paying clients access to your calendar at *their* convenience and your volunteer cases access to your calendar at *your* convenience. Be sure to let the volunteer cases know that you can more quickly accommodate their case if they would like to move from the no-pay category to the for-pay category.

If your practice falls into the for pay bracket, you'll want to research what your market can bear. What do the attorneys in your area charge hourly, what do the other providers charge, and is this fee appropriate for the service your practice provides? You might want to run some numbers that speak to your own bottom line needs. Keep in mind that most Westerners believe that they get what they pay for. If you charge little or nothing for your services, then you relay to the consumer that your service is worthless.

PROMOTION

Promotion involves those various methods of touching or contacting your target market to make them aware of your practice. Promotion may include advertisements, public relations, special promotions etc.

PERCEPTION

How your target market perceives your practice may be more important than any other factor in your marketing. It doesn't matter whether or not you provide the best service in town if your target market thinks someone else does. Every time you answer the phone you give your prospect a perceived idea about the level of service you offer. Each and every piece of direct mail, e-mail, print media and Internet media makes an impact that creates a perception about your practice. Keep this "P" on the top your mind with each and every contact.

POSITIONING

Read this "P" as differentiation. Determine your particular position by differing from your competition. Start by looking at your geographic location, your target market, their industry preferences (psychographics), other service providers (your competition) and your particular background and experience. These descriptive categories will help you establish your particular niche.

PROFESSIONAL HELP

Lots of beginners think that they can do all of their marketing and advertising themselves but smart business people know that hiring professionals is an investment in their future profits. Focus on YOUR core competencies and utilize the skills of others to improve your position.

PLANNING

Planning is probably the cheapest insurance you can buy. Without it you'll be running your practice on a wing and a prayer – not the most pragmatic or enviable position for anyone serious about owning a business.

PERSONNEL

Train all personnel (including yourself) who interact with the public. Lack of courtesy is the biggest single reason people stop doing business with a provider. Your personnel are a direct reflection of your credibility, professionalism and business mission. Train them well.

PRODUCT (SERVICE) KNOWLEDGE

If you don't have a complete understanding of your service – how can you possibly sell it? Knowledge of your service should be available to prospects in clear and brief verbal explanations, written material, etc. that shows the clear benefit to the client, the niche of your practice, or what's unusual about your practice.

POLICIES

Establishing policies for dealing with your clients is an important aspect to providing a consistent performance. Your policies will make dealing with your clients much easier for you both. You can save money and avoid client dissatisfaction (and create a great source of referral) by installing some simple policies like fee schedules that include cancellation policies, travel policies, and the percentage of pro bono cases your practice will carry.

PROFITABILITY

Profit is the sole, sane reason to be in business. You may have other worthwhile goals of a charitable or social nature, but unless you make a profit you cannot achieve those goals. Marketing and market research are your best investments in future profits. If you know who your customers are and what they want from your practice – the probability of profitability goes up drastically.

PRIORITIES

Marketing is complex. Like a puzzle, many small and large pieces must come together seamlessly. In order to accomplish this you must set priorities to assure continued progress toward your goals. Some activities must be done prior to others or are of higher importance to reaching those goals. The main idea is to make sure that the important activities are done first.

PREPARATION

The Boy Scouts have the right idea – "Be Prepared". Marketing is too important to be left to the last minute and ad hoc solutions. Plan ahead by using the Business Plan Template and Marketing Plan Template to outline your activities. Augment these tools by creating a

Communication Plan (see chapter 7) and following through the campaign activities you'll outline for yourself.

POIGNANCY

Identify the hot buttons for your target market as well as the hot buttons for ADR. For many practitioners emotions will be the key and for others the bottom line will be a primary concern. Either way, remember that most choices to hire a provider are made by an individual who can be affected by the poignant words and ads.

THE FOUR PS WORKSHEET

Use the space below to fill in your current strategy for each of the "Ps" listed. Once you've completed this book you may want to come back and redefine your answers.

PRODUCT:

_____

_____

_____

_____

_____

_____

PLACE:

_____

_____

_____

_____

_____

_____

PRICE:

_____

_____

_____

_____

_____

_____

PROMOTION:

_____
_____
_____
_____
_____
_____
_____

PERCEPTION:

_____
_____
_____
_____
_____
_____
_____

POSITIONING:

_____
_____
_____
_____
_____
_____
_____

PROFESSIONAL HELP:

_____
_____
_____
_____
_____

PLANNING:

_____
_____
_____
_____
_____
_____

PERSONNEL:

_____
_____
_____
_____
_____
_____

PRODUCT (SERVICE) KNOWLEDGE:

_____
_____
_____
_____
_____
_____

POLICIES:

_____
_____
_____
_____
_____

PROFITABILITY:

_____
_____
_____
_____
_____
_____

PRIORITIES:

_____
_____
_____
_____
_____
_____

PREPARATION:

_____
_____
_____
_____
_____
_____

POIGNANCY:

_____
_____
_____
_____

Marketing Myths & Truths

▼ ▼ ▼

"In the factory we make cosmetics. In the store we sell hope."
Charles Revlon

Myth   1

Sell the sizzle and not the steak.

Truth   1

Sell the solution and not the sizzle. The easiest way to sell a product is to offer it as the solution to a problem. If you tend to look for the sizzle rather than the problem, you are looking in the wrong direction. Your prospects might appreciate the sizzle, but they'll write a check for the solution. Do all in your power to identify problems that your prospects have then position your service as the best solution to that problem.

If you think solutions, you'll market solutions. If you think sizzle, you'll sell sizzle. These days, people love sizzle as much as ever. But given a choice of purchasing sizzle or a solution with their discretionary income, customers will put their money on the solution every time.

When you present your practice as a solution, you follow the path of least resistance to the sale.

Myth 2

Great marketing works instantly.

Truth 2

Great marketing does NOT work instantly. Marketing a practice is a process – not an event. Great marketing is made up of creating a desire for your service in the minds of qualified prospects over time. This is especially true of ADR consumers. They won't hire you unless they like you and trust you and the only way they'll know if they like and trust you is to get to know you over time.

Myth 3

Marketing should be changed every few years to keep it fresh and new.

Truth 3

The longer great marketing promotes a service, the better. Successful marketers create marketing strategies with which they can live for five to ten years or longer. How long do you suppose the Green Giant has been jolly? How long have people been in good hands with Allstate? Do you think these firms would have been more successful if they kept changing their marketing around to keep it fresh and new? I think not.

Myth 4

Bad publicity is better than no publicity at all.

Truth 4

Bad publicity is bad for your business. No publicity is a lot healthier for you. People love to gossip, especially about businesses that have done something so bad that it got written up in the paper or exposed on the TV news. That's why bad word of mouth spreads so rapidly.

Perhaps for a no-name politician seeking any kind of publicity, bad publicity is better than none – simply for the sake of name recognition. But I'm not too sure about that. I am sure, though, that bad publicity is something that gives no joy to any self-respecting marketer.

Did you know…..? On average, a positive recommendation will be made only 10 times and a negative recommendation will be made 50 times.

Myth 5

Word-of-mouth marketing is all a great business needs.

Truth 5

Amazingly, some otherwise well-informed arbitrators and mediators believe this myth to be true. Here and now, I implore you to understand that it is hardly ever true.

How will consumers know enough about you to spread the word in the first place? Marketing is the answer. How will people hear of the small business when it is new? Marketing is how. Where will the people come from – those who will make all the referrals? They will come from marketing.

It is true that great marketing can attract so many people to a great business that word-of-mouth marketing is active and effective. But that takes time. It takes coddling of customers, customers who came in because of marketing. And anyhow, that customer coddling is marketing.

I have had a few clients who were able to discontinue their marketing because they reached the limits of their growth. But I have witnessed others who thought they could discontinue marketing only to find that a competitor took their customers away from them.

A good marketing campaign demands that you offer so much quality and service that word-of-mouth marketing becomes one of your most efficient tools. It should always be part of your marketing, and you should do all in your power to encourage and promote it. But I do not recommend that you rely on it solely. The bankruptcy courts are littered with businesses that felt they could save on marketing by leaving everything to word-of-mouth. Business just doesn't work that way.

Myth 6

Quality is the main determinant in influencing consumers.

Truth   6

Quality is second most important determinant in influencing sales. Confidence in the business is the main determinant. Nobody wants to hire the best provider if it comes along with the poorest service. People aren't interested in quality if they have to sacrifice self-esteem. Just as word-of-mouth marketing is an integral part of marketing –but not the only part – quality service is the key element to your success – but not the only element.

Customer service must also be present. A friendly attitude must be displayed. The customer must be singled out as special. That customer should be provided with a selection, with convenience, with flexibility in paying for the purchase, with the feeling of a good value. Prospects become customers of businesses that offer credibility – in décor, attire, displays, marketing, employees, and especially in their reputation for offering value. Those items *plus* quality influence sales. Unfortunately, quality alone won't do the job.

Myth   7

Repetition of a marketing message is boring.

Truth   7

It may be boring to you, but it won't be boring to your prospects and customers. Repetition implants your benefits in the unconscious minds of your prospects, and reaffirms those benefits in the conscious minds of your customers. Repetition does not bore these wonderful people.

The Magic Bullet ▼ ▼ ▼

"To open a shop is easy, to keep it open is an art."
Confucius

In a free-association game with service providers, the most common response to the word "marketing" was "advertising". The most common response to "advertising" was "sales", and the most common response to "sales" was "car salesmen" and "telemarketing". When we then asked them how they felt about these two final responses, they let us know that they associated marketing with the "slick" maneuvering of car salesmen and the untimely and interruptive abilities of telemarketers. Two professions they would never aspire to be a part of.

In short, they were uncomfortable with the task of marketing their practices and more importantly, they thought that their prospective clients would view them as equals to the "slick" salesmen they themselves didn't like. Practitioners told us they were quite comfortable with what they were doing in their own Alternative Dispute Resolution (ADR) practice, law firm or career of choice that had segued into an ADR practice, but that they had no education or experience with marketing. They didn't feel qualified to promote themselves, so they choose not to promote themselves at all. Instead, most hoped that once they received their ADR education, new business would find it's way to them.

This method of marketing does not work.

It especially does not work for arbitrators and mediators. As arbitrators and mediators, we are concerned with maintaining our neutrality and surpassing the codes of conduct and rules of ethics we impose upon ourselves. We expect that members of our industry will conduct themselves to the highest possible standard. We are, after all, professional negotiators, facilitators, communicators, listeners, and peacemakers.

So let's think about how we, as mediators and arbitrators think of ourselves when we are marketing or selling our services. First, do we exaggerate by telling everyone we encounter that we can solve their problems? Do we mislead our clients and end users? No, we sell just the opposite—confidentiality, trust and honorability. As an industry, we take ethics very seriously and attempt to dissolve bias at every turn. Then why do we feel cheap when we talk about marketing such a noble industry?

Perhaps mediators and arbitrators need to change their schema of marketers and marketing. We regularly use tools like outstanding customer service, educational opportunities, and community interaction to provide awareness. We market our services every time we answer the phone, and answer a question about our industry or our particular practice.

ADR, in its various forms, serves as an answer to so many of our social, judicial, and personal ailments. Selling a product of this nature should be easy, a pleasure, and a top priority for practitioners.

Marketing and selling is more than just direct mail, brochures, and Web sites. Marketing and selling is instilling trust and confidence, those virtues we extol as ADR professionals, in our clients and the larger population. When we address our potential clients and society in general, we represent not just our own practice, but the entire ADR industry. One poor experience with an ADR provider may be all it takes to send a consumer back to the default justice of litigation. Take the time to think about how you represent yourself and our industry – market us with honor and enjoyment.

As folks who pride ourselves on providing solutions, not problems; comfort, not discontent; and hope, not dismay, how can we promote and market ourselves without abusing the expected standards of conduct for our industry and violating the trust of potential clients?

What does work?

What is the magic bullet that will propel your practice into success? Most marketing experts will tell you that there is no magic bullet; they tell you instead that marketing is a complex, difficult, many-layered task that requires years of experience and education. Well… as it turns out, I happen to think they're wrong.

There is a magic bullet.

There is a magic bullet that anyone with any amount of education or experience can employ for success. A magic bullet that is so simple and so obvious that most of you reading this book won't believe it until you've tried it. And if you've already tried it, then you know I'm right.

So what is the ultimate marketing tool, the perfect answer to all questions, the definitive technique for transforming your practice?

Well, before I answer that, let's go back a bit.

When I was a little girl, my father had a tee-shirt that read "No man is completely worthless. He can always serve as a bad example." Well that's what the typical car salesman and telemarketer can do for you (my apologies to all the car salesmen and telemarketers who have done a very fine job at their chosen profession – and there are many of you).

The important question here is *why*. What is it about their techniques we're uncomfortable with? Why do we bristle at their strategies to get us to buy? Why do we view marketing with such trepidation (we're professional communicators for goodness's sake)? So what can they teach us?

Let's start with auto sales. Think about how you feel when you're engaged in a conversation with a salesman on a car lot. Do you feel comfortable with your automotive knowledge? Are you confident that you will be able to negotiate the best possible deal for yourself? Though there are a few people who actually enjoy negotiating for and purchasing their cars, most of us do not. More often we feel at a disadvantage because we lack the technical auto information the salesman seems to so easily spew forth, and we're being put in a spot to trust the very person whom we hold suspect to owning all kinds of undesirable attributes. We frequently feel like we're not in control of the buying process. We feel like we're being played and manipulated for someone else's enjoyment and profit. Something we certainly don't want our potential clients to feel.

And how about the telemarketer? Why do we view telemarketing as such a loathsome practice? No matter where he's calling from or on which topic he is speaking, he can always find the time in our day when we are the most occupied, and attempt to sell us a product that we would never use. We regard his nerve and audacity with disgust. Many of us reply with negative words that equal the heat of a supernova. Others of us just drop the phone back into its cradle and go on with our task at hand. The last thing in the world we want from out prospects is that kind of response.

Just as one bad experience with a car salesman or telemarketer imbues their entire industry with self-serving interests that we find so offensive, one poor experience of a disputant with an ADR provider will imbue our whole profession with mistrust.

So how do we avoid being viewed as we view them?

Read on.

Ah … the magic bullet.

You must serve before you sell. This sentiment is so important to your success that it bears repeating. You must serve before you sell.

The magic bullet to success is to serve before you sell.

Serve before you sell. It sounds so simple – and it is.

Arbitrators and mediators, by definition, are service providers. We don't sell a tangible product. We sell a service. We provide a much-needed service to every type of industry and individual for nearly every situation involving a dispute. We must everyday remember that our clients choose us. We are not the default – that's the court system, we are the alternative. And in order to be chosen we must provide not just a better product, but we must provide it with smile.

When you serve before you sell you show your prospect that you have their best interests in mind and that it's important to you to provide them a quality service.

For instance, if someone calls your office looking for general information about the benefits of mediation in the employment industry, you should do the best you can to verbally describe the process and its benefits. You might then follow up with an appropriate article via mail, e-mail, or fax. Let them know that you'll call them back to discuss any questions or concerns they have about ADR in general, or your services in particular. Provide them with a referral if one is necessary and can be made.

Serving before you sell allows your prospects to get to know you and the level of service they can expect to receive from your practice. Make each prospect feel like they're getting special attention from you.

SWOT Analysis

A SWOT analysis is one way to help you make wise choices in choosing marketing strategies for your practice. SWOT stands for Strengths, Weaknesses, Opportunities, and Threats. The idea is that you capitalize on your strengths and bolster your weaknesses. Therefore, use this tool to maximize your opportunities and minimize any threats to increase your probability of success.

Your SWOT analysis should begin by looking internally. Evaluate your internal strengths and weaknesses in the areas of quality, customer service, profitability, marketing, financial resources and management, and operations. If you have a support staff or associates who could help shed some light on your internal strengths and weaknesses – don't ignore them. They are frequently a fantastic source of information and insight you should use to your advantage.

You next need to look at the external aspects of your practice like the geographic region in which you operate. Also take into account your current customers, the kinds of customers you'd like to have, your competition, the technology at your disposal, the political climate of your area, any regulatory bodies that will impact your practice, the legal environment and the current economy.

Pick no more than five strengths and opportunities to focus on, and no more than five weaknesses and threats to concern yourself with. Choose carefully. This is the time in which you will create the focus of your practice.

Understanding your strengths and weaknesses will help you pinpoint your marketing strategies. For instance: Do you have a specialty or area of expertise? Is competition rife in your market? What you want to work out is what you should focus on, which small niche you might be able to create and dominate, and how you could serve your clients better than your competition.

Every provider has some competition. The trick is to identify which ones pose a threat and which ones don't. If you're a sole proprietor whose specialty is employment, then other local providers with the same specialty are your direct competition. If you're interested in creating a national panel of attorneys and judges to hear cases, then the Mediator Network, the American Arbitration Association and JAMS are your competition.

SWOT ANALYSIS WORKSHEET

Five Strengths and Opportunities

1. _____
2. _____
3. _____
4. _____
5. _____

Five Weaknesses and Threats

1. _____
2. _____
3. _____
4. _____
5. _____

Determining Your Target Market

▼ ▼ ▼

Whenever you see a successful business,
someone once made a courageous decision."
Peter Drucker

Mediators and arbitrators, when determining the goals and aspirations
of their practices, need to consider whether their practice will be one
of a specialized or generalized nature. The arguments go both ways
(and usually loudly).

Many practitioners (as well and advocates and their clients) are under
the opinion that anyone with court approved training in the processes
of ADR can hear any kind of case under the sun. Most of these folks
reason that if a practitioner fully understands the processes of ADR,
the content of the hearing is moot - that their communication skills
will allow them to lead the parties to a settlement or that their common sense or their understanding of the law will allow them to rule
appropriately.

The other side of the argument goes something like this. In a world where every aspect of our lives is evolving toward a specialist's society, ranging from physicians to real estate, and from construction to psychotherapy, ADR practitioners should follow suit. That a case based in a subject of complexity will require a provider with a background that allows them to understand the details presented to them. In effect, they should speak the language of the parties, as well as have a deep understanding of the ADR process.

Both have valid points. Both are usually adamant about their opinion. And both can become successful in the field of Alternative (or Appropriate) Dispute Resolution.

However, …

From a practice-development point of view, and after working with 100's of clients worldwide, I can tell you that it is much easier to promote a specialty or niche practice, and here's why:

▶ If you've had a long or distinguished career that has earned you the respect of your peers, you're a much easier "sell" to your target market than to a target market who knows nothing about you or your background.

▶ You therefore garner more respect with little regard to the attorney vs. non-attorney status.

▶ You can easily identify your target market.

▶ You can more easily identify your target market's needs and concerns, as well as being more in tune to various underlying issues.

▶ You probably already belong to the right associations and organizations or have served them in some capacity, which will allow you a faster rate of acceptance within your target market.

All in all, as a marketing representative of ADR providers around the globe I recommend staying within your field of expertise.

For those providers whose background does not provide them a singular and powerful presence in their target market, choose a niche within the ADR industry that is related to some specific portion of your resume, and begin to establish yourself as the premier provider for that selected target market.

To understand target marketing you should think about everyone, everywhere who could possibly be interested in hiring you. The mental list you just made is your total or global market. Your list probably included attorneys, individuals, business professionals, counselors and therapists, etc. Now, in order for these folks to hire you, they have to know your practice even exists, that you can provide your service at a competitive price, that you're convenient to them, and all of this must be done to their satisfaction. However, o f the total market you just created you can probably only afford to reach a small percentage.

The folks in your total market who can afford your services, are most willing to hire you, and are accessible to you are your real target market.

So how do you know who they are? Common sense combined with a little market research should make the beginnings of your target market focus or niche. To continue refining your focus, look to trade sources that can tell you about the individuals you intend to market to as well as their demographics, geographic location, reading preferences and their reasons for hiring ADR professionals.

If you have a specialty practice you have to choose a niche that is large enough for you to grow and make a profit, yet small enough to defend against newcomers. (Remember that your best defense is customer service).

Ask yourself if your niche meets these simple criteria. If so, you're on the right track, if not, keep searching.

A market niche is a small fragment of a larger market. You can choose your niche in a variety of ways. The best way is to pick a niche that seems to be underserved by the ADR industry and fits within your spectrum of specialized experiences.

Target marketing doesn't imply that you focus on a single niche alone. You can identify multiple niches that fit within a larger target market. For instance instead of saying that your niche is family disputes, design a practice that deals with a specific aspect of family life. Your practice could focus on parent/teen relationships, adult children and their elderly parents, you might even go so far as to specialize in those disputes that arise from engagements and wedding planning.

The decision to approach multiple niches should not be taken lightly. It costs more and takes more time. It is much easier to be a force in a single niche than a force in several.

You might also consider with whom you prefer working. More likely than not you have some clients who are a sheer joy to work with, who trust your judgment, appreciate your skills and happily spread the word about your practice. Study those clients and find more of them. According to Pareto's principle, 80 percent of your profits come from 20 percent of your clients. Why not focus on this 20 percent and seek more them. Forget about the 80 percent who bring more headaches than they're worth.

You might be able to determine your niche simply by paying attention to the trends of your current practice. If one part of your market is growing, you should concentrate your efforts on that niche and grow with it. On the other hand, if one segment of your market is shrinking, consider abandoning it.

Keep in mind the old adage ~ It is almost always better to be a big fish in a little pond than a little fish in Lake Superior. Big fish in the little ponds eat better.

Understanding the perceptions of your target market is the goal of your market research. This research shouldn't be too expensive and if you're somewhat creative you can compile what you need at no charge. Your goal is to learn what motivates your target market toward purchasing ADR services. An important note here – every person who attends a hearing is your client. Make a list of all the parties. Then using some generalizations ask yourself the following questions about each participant.

- Who are these people? What is their demographic and psychographic profile?

- When do they purchase? As soon as a dispute arises, upon advice from family, friends or clergy, prior to litigation or during the litigation process?

- How do they shop for your service? From a trusted source of referral, direct marketing, in the Yellow Pages or on the Internet?

- How do they like to pay? Cash, check or charge?

- Why do they purchase your service? Why from you or why not from you?

- How can you differentiate yourself from the competition? What makes you different in *their eyes – not yours*?

- Most important of all: What do your clients and prospects perceive to be the value of your service? Do they cherish fast-track hearings, courteous service, customized processes, the ability to pay with a credit card?

Then provide it. Success follows.

Positioning ▼ ▼ ▼

"To be successful, you must not follow strategies that your top competitor is pursuing; if you try to be someone else, the best you can be is second best."
Sun Tzu, The Art of War

Traditionally, strategy involves broad decisions about who you want to appeal to, how you will position yourself, and so on. Tactics are specific ways of implementing strategy. As mentioned at the beginning of this book; that is the most important strategic decision you can make about your marketing.

The growth of mediation and arbitration has changed the process of choosing a provider. Consumers have much more knowledge about ADR processes and the kinds of providers they want. It is usual for sources of referral to provide prospects just one name. This is important since it's not uncommon for parties and counsel to shop around for a provider.

This is when a clear positioning statement can differentiate your practice.

Al Ries and Jack Trout in their book "Positioning" suggest that in order to create a positioning strategy you need to answer their six simple questions. These questions are easy to ask, tough to answer and may require a bit of soul-searching and courage.

1. "What position do you own? Positioning is thinking is reverse. Instead of starting with yourself, you start with the mind of the prospects.

2. What position do you want to own?

3. Whom must you outgun?

4. Do you have enough money?

5. Can you stick it out?

6. Do you match your position?"

"Benjamin Franklin may have discovered electricity, but it was the man who invented the meter who made the money."
Earl Wilson

Let me tell you the story of a service provider who found more success than he could imagine simply by repositioning himself. A family friend here in Los Angeles has been a structural engineer for more than 30 years. He worked and struggled in this very competitive industry to build himself a small but profitable firm. He had several assistants and draftsmen. And in this modern era of computer-aided engineering, he has remained true to his art and provides his clients detailed, delicate, hand-rendered specifications. Although his skills and talents are vast and great, he was loathe to charge more than his competitors for fear of losing the business he had so carefully cultivated.

One night at a dinner party he was lamenting that although his firm had grown, his
personal profit had remained nearly the same, and in fact, he was spending even more time away from his family since he not only had more jobs but also many more staff to manage. He was considering closing his firm and taking an early retirement. Well, my father (from whom I have learned most of my negotiation skills) made a simple suggestion that moved this hard-working man and his practice into the top 1% of his field.

His suggestion was this: Let go of your draftsmen and assistants.

My father advised, "Next time a potential client calls your office, let them know that your calendar is booked, you have more work than you can handle, but that for a *rush fee* you might be able to *consider* their project." Now, since our friend would be letting go his staff, the statement wasn't a falsehood.

He next suggested that the price for a set of drawings should be raised – raised to a level of the top 10% of fee schedules in our area. His reasoning is that people expect to get what they pay for. If you charge a minimum fee, folks assume they will get a minimum service (i.e. if you charge a competitive fee, they assume they will get a competitive service.)

Our friend more than doubled his prices and let go his staff and high overhead. He asked his wife to help him in his newly obtained two-room office. She was instructed to let potential clients know that he was already overbooked, but as a personal favor to them, she would ask her husband to consider their project (at a much greater fee, of course). She is an artist in her own right when it comes to creating a sense of urgency and demand for her husband's drawings.

Within the first year of their transition, our friends had made more money than in the past decade's history of their now defunct firm. They were finally able to travel internationally and visit their children and grandchildren at their leisure. They have moved out of their tract home in the suburbs and built their dream home in Beverly Hills.

They work less and earn more. They charge more and play more.

Our friend and his wife have created a thriving practice simply by establishing the perception that he was the best and most sought after. If you want the best structural engineer in the area (and trust me, in LA, you do) then you pay the price, take a number, and wait on line.

He truly IS one of the very best, and his fees now reflect his skills.

From a marketing standpoint, it's all about perception. The perception of the general public is that they will get what they pay for.

That's one example of positioning. There are many. You can position yourself in ways other than price.

Your personal values or the values you imbue your practice with might be appropriate (e.g. peace, empowerment, closure). You can also consider your lifestyle, culture, political philosophies, or religious preferences. Some very important positioning points will be your practice specialty like employment, family, construction, etc. Do you favor facilitative or evaluative (maybe a combination of the two)? Do you practice from an emotional position or a business position? Do you have stringent or flexible office hours?

Most marketers will tell you that being first to market is key. Well … no big news here that you're not the first ADR provider. However, you might be able to be a first in your area with your chosen specialty to offer flexible office hours. Again, if you follow in someone's positioning footsteps, the best you can be is second to market. You might eventually become better known, but why fight an uphill battle.

Differentiate yourself from the competition. The old cliché that you fight fire with fire is silly. You fight fire with water. Take advantage of the position that your direct competition does not. The French have saying that sums this up nicely "cherchez le creneau" or look for the hole. Look for the hole – then fill it.

THE NAME GAME

A key component in positioning is choosing a name for yourself. Since we've already determined that you can't be all things to all people you have to choose a name that summarizes who you are, how you provide your service, or with what belief systems.

A name should be short, easy to say, and easy to spell. Alliteration is a powerful tool in naming (e.g. Mosten Mediation). A name should be positive, active, and show a benefit. How can all of these attributes be put into a name that deals with a negative industry? Just flip the negative around. Instead of naming your company Dispute Specialists try Solution Specialists. Instead of Employment Dispute Resolution try Employment Empowerment. You get the idea – dwell on the positive and say what you do.

Many providers who have already solidly established themselves in an industry don't necessarily need a name. For instance Allan Matt of Matt Construction is highly regarded in the construction industry. At the beginning of his practice if he chooses a name like Construction Conciliation he will in essence be throwing aside the respect and reputation he has spent decades building. A more powerful name for him to use would be Allan Matt Mediation. His prospects will recognize his name and associate his mediation practice with his construction experience.

However, if the folks in your target market aren't familiar with you don't fall into the no name trap. Let your business name do the talking.

Marketing is a Contact Sport

COMMUNICATION PLAN™

Make no bones about it, marketing is a contact sport. If you don't contact your clients and prospective clients regularly you don't play and if you don't play, you can't win.

In marketing terminology, those contacts are called "touches" or impressions. If it sounds "familiar" it should be just that. You want your target to become familiar with you and your practice. In order to accomplish this you must first familiarize yourself with their preferences and personalities (see the chapter on creating a niche for yourself).

It is absolutely critical that a plan of communicating with your target market is created prior to embarking on any marketing activities. I want that to sink in with you so let me say that again. It is absolutely critical that a plan of communicating with your target market is created prior to embarking on any marketing activities.

The reason is simple; you must *PLAN PLAN PLAN*. Flying by the seat of your pants is not only unfathomably expensive; it is also one of the major reasons providers go out of business. However, if you know where your practice is in terms of case load and annual revenues and you know where you would like to take your practice, then the single best way to achieve the end result is to lay out a plan of attack, then work your way backwards to reach your goals.

I have seen a number of different ways to accomplish this. There is what I call the "MBA way" and by this I mean a very complicated method that takes into account complex algorithmic models that pinpoint the number of target market impressions reached down to a 99.5% confidence interval that can be translated into bottom line number. Then there is what I refer to as the "Mom & Pop" method, which can be as simple as handing out ice cream to the exiting customers of an appliance store selling freezers.

Of course these examples are located at opposite ends of the spectrum. But I find that a combination of the two will work just fine for our purposes here and a good medium can be found in what I call a Communication Plan™.

While the Communication Plan™ is essentially designed to plan out the who, when, what, where, and how of reaching your target market, it is also plays two additional critical roles. If properly used, the Communication Plan™ will provide you with a marketing budgeting tool and a time management outline. The combination of all of these tools that equates to what I call business intelligence.

Business intelligence is absolutely critical to increasing your probability of success.

What do I mean by this? Let's take a closer look at the Communication Plan™ to obtain a better understanding.

Communication Plan™ is a comprehensive plan outlying the methods used to reach one's unique target market by combining the appropriate marketing mediums and the appropriate time lines into a single cohesive plan. Taking into consideration one's available marketing budget and the their target market's preferences.

To begin with, the average prospective client requires between six and eight touches or impressions to convert from a prospect to a client. This is accomplished by working to build "mindshare" within your target market. So what is mindshare?

Mindshare is the idea that when a dispute arises, a prospective client will think of you first. This greatly increases the probability that you will be contacted first. Think about it this way: If a majority of your target market, upon realizing that they needed your services, contacted you first could this ultimately increase your case load? Mindshare is priceless.

Let's look at some other everyday examples:

- ▸ Soft drinks: Who comes to mind? Coke, Sprite, Dr. Pepper?
- ▸ How about computing software: Microsoft?
- ▸ When you think of an airline: Who's first American, Delta, United'?
- ▸ When you think about fast food restaurants: Is it MacDonald's, Burger King or Taco Bell first?

The first service provider to enter a prospective client's mind is going to be in the best position to convert that prospect into a client every single time.

So how do you achieve mindshare? By using your Communication Plan™ and how does a Communication Plan™ work?

The ultimate goal of the Communication Plan™ is to help you reach your target market no closer together than 4 weeks and no further apart than 6 weeks. If touches are too close together, your prospects will feel hounded or harassed. If your touches are too far apart your prospects will begin to forget you from the last touch and you'll loose valuable mindshare. But hit the timing just right every time and you will begin to build mindshare. The Communication Plan™ accomplishes this by keeping to a strict calendar schedule.

I cannot too heartily prevail upon the importance of consistency in your marketplace. You have to be where your customers are when they need you. You can't assume that your target market will always have a need for your service the precise moment you place an ad or send a letter. You must create mindshare with consistent impressions. You simply cannot deviate from the plan and expect to reach the same levels of success.

The touches you choose should use a variety of mediums to relay your marketing message unless your prospects have a clear preference for one form of communication over another. You will want to alternate between e-mail, direct mail, faxes, phone calls, speeches, etc.

In order to create a Communication Plan™ you will want to look ahead in yearly increments. Take out your current calendar and next year's as well. On these calendars you will plot out your marketing activities, deadlines, holidays to keep in mind, reasons for contact, and industry preferences. For instance sending your materials to an accountant from January through April will be a waste of your time and money. You want to market your services to your target market when they have time to listen to your message.

On the same calendar you need to list to whom you will be marketing, what the intended message will contain, and via what medium it will be conveyed. The content should be customized to fit your goals, your potential client's goals, economic, legal and industry trends, and holidays.

USING THE COMMUNICATION PLAN™

Using the Communication Plan™ is essential to your success. Why? Here are two great case studies.

A provider called me one day and was really excited that he had done so much work towards getting his marketing program started. He had purchased a database of 5,500 qualified prospects at the cost of $0.75 per name. He hired a graphic artist to create a tri-fold brochure for a design fee of $3,000.00, then went out and commissioned a local printer to print the brochures. Because he was budget conscious, he took advantage of the price cuts that the printer offered and was able to lower his per brochure print cost by 20% by ordering 50,000 brochures to a total of $28,000. In preparation for his direct mailing, he then spent $160.00 in LaserJet mailing labels and $50.00 in toner cartridges. He decided to hire a local college student to apply 5,500 $0.34 stamps and 5,500 labels at $8.00/per hour. It took the student four full days to apply 5,500 stamps, for a total direct labor cost of $256.00. After the 5,500 tri-fold brochures were disseminated he received a 1% rate of response from the mailing (average). Which means that 55 people called him back looking for more information. Of the 55 warm leads, he was able to convert 5% into paying cases. Each of the three cases yielded an average of $1,650.00 in revenue.

Let's look at the bottom line results:

Total Revenue:	$ 4,950.00
Total Expenses:	$ 37,498.50
Profit/<Loss>:	<$ 32,548.50>

Dilemma: 44,500 brochures remaining, budget is zero.

Had he used a Communication Plan™ he would have planned differently (*not by the seat of his pants*) and his results could have looked something like this.

TOUCH   1: Direct Mail Piece of Tri-Fold Brochure

1-Time cost of database: $4,125
1-Time cost of graphic artist: $3,000
Printing for only 5,500 brochures @ $0.67 each: $3,696.00
Laser labels & toner: $210.00
Postage: $1,870
College student: $256.00

Rate or response: 1% (same as scenario # 1 mailing) or 55 prospects
Total prospects converted: 5% or 3 cases.

Total Revenue: $ 4,950.00
Total Expenses: $ 13,157.00
Profit/<Loss>:   <$ 8,207.00>

TOUCH   2: Internet Newsletter

Cost of database: $0.00 (since he already owns it)
Opportunity cost to compose newsletter: 4 hours @ $125.00 per hour = $500.00
Cost to send our 5,500 newsletters via email: $0.00

Rate of Response: .001% or 5.5 prospects.
Total prospects converted 18%: 1

Total Revenue: $ 1,650.00
Total Expenses: $ 500.00
Profit/<Loss>: $ 1,150.00

TOUCH   3: Networking Touch

Costs of joining three target market associations in his area: $300.00
Opportunity cost of speaking at each networking event and spending nine hours of networking time at the punch bowl over the course of three events at $125.00/hr: $1,125.00
Number of hands he shook and business cards collected: 300

TOUCH   4: Follow-up Letter

Number of follow-up personal letters mailed: 300 at a hard cost of $0.40 each: $120.00

Rate of Response: 35% = 105 prospects interested in his dispute resolution services over the course of the next 4 months

Total prospects converted: 28% = 29 Cases.

Because of the personal contact with these prospects in combination with the mindshare he established with the previous three touches, his conversion rate jumped to 28%. Thus garnering him 29 cases with an average revenue of $1,650.00 per case.

(Touches 3 and 4)

Total Revenue:	$ 47,850.00
Total Expenses:	$ 1,545.00
Profit/<Loss>:	$ 46,305.00

So let's compare scenarios.

Scenario # 1: A one-time, expensive $37,498.50 touch of 5,500 prospects yielding three cases and $4,950.00 in revenue. Ave. = $6.82 per contact.

Vs.

Scenario # 2: A multi-layered set of 11,300 impressions over a four-month period costing a grand total of $15,202, yielding 33 cases, and $54,450 in gross revenue. Ave. = $1.35 per contact.

Following the Communication Plan™ as a road map, our dispute resolution provider would have been able to create a realistic marketing budget tailored specifically to meet his needs. It would have been possible to plan for all the expected costs associated with his marketing efforts and even allow for a 10-15% safety factor in his budget. Knowing that each touch builds mindshare one upon another, he is confident that his rates of response will grow exponentially.

Most conventional marketing and advertising companies will tell you that if you can achieve a .05%- 1.0% rate of return on any single touch or impression that you beat the odds. For a more satisfactory result you combine numerous touches from one cohesive strategy that will enable you to increase your rates of response exponentially not arithmetically. Warning: It is difficult to pre-determine the exponential growth rate of response. Rates of response are based on timing, content, the mood of the recipient, whether or not they like you, whether or not your service is right for them and several other variables. Essentially, what cannot be predetermined is the human element. This is where your new credo of "serve before you sell" comes into play.

Consistent and appropriately frequent touches that have been personalized for your target market will build the mindshare you seek. The Communication Plan™ will lay out the system of touches that accomplish the desired results as they apply to time, money and activities.

So go ahead – reach out and touch someone.

Planning

▼ ▼ ▼

"Long-range planning does not deal with future decisions,
but with the future of present decisions."
Peter F. Drucker

PLAN. PLAN. PLAN.

Pilots file a flight plan, developers require blueprints prior to building, and Generals create battle plans – AND SUCCESSFUL BUSINESSES UTILIZE MARKETING PLANS, BUSINESS PLANS, AND COMMUNICATION PLANS.

Marketing plans do not need to be lengthy, complicated documents that require a decoder ring to understand. Most ADR practices are small firms or sole proprietors that need a marketing plan that is simple and inexpensive to implement. Below are the bare necessities for a marketing plan. For expansion on these points look at the marketing plan template in the Appendix.

SEVEN CRITICAL ELEMENTS
OF YOUR MARKETING PLAN

1. The benefit to consumers

2. Your positioning in the marketplace: What business are you in?

3. Your target market

4. Your advertising strategy and positioning

5. Your budget

6. The tools and techniques you'll use to reach your audience

7. A month-by-month implementation timetable

THE NUMBER ONE REASON A GOOD PLAN FAILS: LACK OF COMMITMENT and CONSISTENCY.

Remember, if you don't know where you're going, how will you know when you get there?

Databases

▼ ▼ ▼

"What we see depends mainly on what we look for."
John Lubbock

GATHERING DATA

Database information can be found nearly everywhere you look. You can gather information about your prospective clients from organizations and associations that support your target market. Most have membership lists that can be purchased for nominal fees. Another source, the Internet, is a vast resource of information about your target market. Try a couple of our favorite search engines like www.Google.com, or www.AltaVista.com. Collecting business cards and/or lists from your local Chamber of Commerce is easy enough and the old standby, the Yellow Pages, is another way to amass contacts (your public library will have all the phone books for your region).

You can always purchase a ready-made or customized list of contacts. Mail list companies usually charge between $0.20 to $1.33 per contact and offer a deliverability rate of between 80% and 95%. The

prices will vary from company to company as well as the amount of information you require. For instance if you need just names and addresses then the price may be $0.40 per contact. If you ask for names, company names, addresses, phone and fax numbers and email addresses, then you may pay slightly more. And if you need even more information like where your contact went to college, their birth dates, etc. the prices can skyrocket.

The point here is data is everywhere.

Marketers need a focused and accurate database that is as large as is appropriate for your region, your industry and your business goals.

Think of every customer as an individual, not as a mass-market statistic. Database marketers make the extra effort to learn about their customers' individual needs, interests and desires. They create relationships based on what they've learned and market to those same individuals over and over again.

MANAGING YOUR DATABASE

Whether you use a simple Rolodex card system or invest a small amount in a computerized contact management software program (our favorite is Goldmine – you can try it out at www.Goldmine.com or www.FrontRange.com), you need to be able to keep accurate records. The goal of database marketing is to discover what your customers need and want and make it easy for them to obtain it. While computers and software can make this job easier – they may also make a simple task more complex than some providers need it to be. If you

can make do with index cards, that's fine. Don't let the complexity and cost of a computer system stop you from getting started.

BEST UTILIZATION OF YOUR DATABASE

A database is a valuable resource and usually held close the to the vest. Your database can be used not only for names and addresses but also for determining trends in the industry by monitoring the attrition rate. You can use your database to refine your marketing plan activities. For instance, by paying attention to what percentage of the business cards collected have an e-mail address you may decide that an e-mail campaign is either your best bet or a waste of time.

DATABASE WORKSHEET

Harvey Mackey, the author of, "Swim With the Sharks Without Being Eaten Alive"; (1988), Ballantine Books suggests using the following customer profile when compiling a database.

Customer Profile

Date:
Last Update:
By:

CUSTOMER

1. Name:
    Nickname:
    Title:

2. Company Name and Address:

3. Home Address:

4. Contact Numbers

       Business:
       Home:
       Cell:
       Pager:
       Fax:
       E-mail:

5. Birth Date and Place:
    Hometown:

6. Height:
    Weight:
    Outstanding Physical Characteristics:

EDUCATION

1. High School and Year:
    College:
    Graduation Date:
    Degrees:

2. College Honors:
    Advanced Degrees:

3. College Fraternity or Sorority:
   Sports:

4. Extra Curricular Activities:

5. If Customer Didn't Attend College, is He/She
   Sensitive About It?
   What Did They Do Instead?

6. Military Service
   Discharge Rank:
   Attitude Toward Being in the Service:

Notes:

_____

_____

_____

_____

_____

FAMILY

1. Marital Status:
   Spouse's Name:

2. Spouse's Education:

3. Spouse's Interests/Activities/Affiliations:

4. Wedding Anniversary:

5. Children, if any, Names and Ages:
    Does Client Have Custody?

6. Children's Education:

7. Children's Interests (Hobbies, Problems, Etc.)

Notes:

_____

_____

_____

_____

_____

BUSINESS BACKGROUND

1. Previous Employment (Most Recent First):
    Company:
    Location:
    Dates:
    Title:

    Company:
    Location:
    Dates:
    Title:

2. Previous Position at Present Company:
    Title:
    Dates:

3. Any "Status"Symbols in Office?

4. Professional or Trade Associations:

5. Any Mentors?

6. What Business Relationship Does He/She Have With Others in our Company?

7. Is It a Good Relationship?
   Why?

8. What Other People in our Company Know the Customer?

9. Type of Connection:
   Nature of Relationship:

10. What is Client's Attitude Toward His/Her Company?

11. What is His/Her Long-Range Business Objective?

12. What is His/Her Immediate Business Objective?

13. What is of Greatest Concern to Customer at this Time: The Welfare of the Company or His/Her Own Personal Welfare?

14. Does the Customer Think of the Present or the Future?
    Why?

Notes:

_____
_____
_____
_____
_____
_____

SPECIAL INTERESTS

1. Clubs or Service Clubs (Masons, Kiwanis, Etc.):

2. Politically Active?
   Party:
   Importance to Customer:

3. Active in Community?
   How?

4. Religion:
   Active?

5. Highly Confidential Items NOT to be Discussed with
   Customer (For Example, Divorce, Member of AA,
   Etc.):

6. On What Subjects (Outside of Business) Does
   Customer Have Strong Feelings?

Notes:

_____

_____

_____

_____

_____

LIFESTYLE

1. Medical History (Current Condition of Health):

2. Does Customer Drink?
    If Yes, What and How Much?

3. If No, Offended by Others Drinking?

4. Does Customer Smoke?
    If No, Object to Others?

5. Favorite Places for Lunch:
    Dinner:

6. Favorite Items on Menu:

7. Does Customer Object to Having Anyone Buy His/
    Her Meal?

8. Hobbies and Recreational Interests:
    What Does Customer Read?

9. Vacation Habits:

10. Spectator-Sports Interest:
    Sports and Teams:

11. Kind of Car(s):

12. Conversational Interests:

13. Whom Does Customer Seem Anxious to Impress:

14. How Does He/She Want to be Seen by Those People:

15. What Adjectives Would You Use to Describe Customer:

16. What is He/She Most Proud of Having Achieved?

17. What Do You Feel is Customer's Long-Range Personal Objective?

18. What Do You Feel is Customer's Immediate Personal Goal?

Notes:

_____

_____

_____

_____

_____

THE CUSTOMER AND YOU

1. What Moral or Ethical Considerations are Involved When You Work with Customer?

2. Does Customer Feel Any Obligation to You, Your Company, or Your Competition?
   If So, What?

3. Does the Proposal You plan to Make to Him/Her Require Customer to Change a Habit or Take an Action that is Contrary to Custom?

4. Is He/She Primarily Concerned About the Opinion of Other?

5. Or Very Self-Centered?
   Highly Ethical?

6. What are the Key Priorities of the Customer's Management?

7. What are the Priorities of the Customer's Management?

8. Any Conflicts Between Customer and Management?

9. Can You Help With These Problems?
   How?

10. Does Your Competitor Have Better Answers to the
Above Questions than You Have?

Direct Mail

▼ ▼ ▼

"Act quickly – think slowly."
Greek proverb

Direct mail is one of the perfect marketing tools. It is targeted, easy
to test and low in cost. It allows you to reach prospects directly,
make your pitch, and invite them to become your client. It is the great
equalizer. Direct mail is just as effective for the large panels and
tribunals as it is for the independent practitioner. In fact, it may be
even more effective for the independent practitioner since a single
provider is willing to have more patience in attracting clients one at a
time.

The key to direct mail lies in testing. You need to constantly test both
your successes and failures. Send out two different pieces to see
which one gets the most response. Testing different wording, different
graphics, and different packaging is a great way to get to know your
target better.

The advantages of direct mail over other media are many.

- ▸ You can measure results more accurately.
- ▸ You can be as expansive or concise as you wish.
- ▸ You can zero in on your target market.
- ▸ You can personalize you marketing.
- ▸ You can compete with the big firms.

The three things to remember in direct mail marketing are the mailing list, the offer, and the packaging.

For more information about the list see the chapter on database construction and management. You need to create or buy a list of your target market with as much specific information as you can find or afford. The more focused (and correct) your list is the more effective your campaign will be.

The offer you make must have a call to action even if it's only for a free consultation. Offering a free service is almost always more effective than trying to sell a service. When you offer a free service you allow your prospects to overcome any concerns or fears about ADR and you can answer their questions in person, which encourages the beginnings of trust that is necessary in ADR.

Direct mail marketing is a fantastic way to contact potential clients and alert them to your services. The tricky part in direct mail is getting recipients to open the piece of mail. There are several ways to get your mailers opened.

Think carefully about the packaging. The more unique, professional, and personalized the piece of mail is, the more likely your recipient is to open it out of curiosity. You should consider the size of your target market and establish a budget (don't forget to include postage). The US Post Office will mail nearly anything with a stamp on it. Use cardboard tubes, 2 x 4s with your information carved into the boards, use priority mail, Fed-Ex — use anything that you think will bring attention to your piece in such a way that it will get opened.

Use colorful stamps that are industry- or time-appropriate, instead of a bulk-mail indicia to send your print media.

The more personalized your piece, the more likely you are to receive a response.

Make it easy for the recipient to contact you — attach a business card to every piece of mail you send.

For additional attention, handwrite a post-script on the piece, on a Post-It note, or on the outside of the mailer (use a colored ink pen and traditional yellow notes so that your recipient knows that you took the time to think about them and them alone). Also, hand-addressed envelopes are opened 72% more often than computer generated addresses.

You should expect a minimal response of 0.005% and a maximum of 2% rate of response. If your mailer falls under the minimum, reformat it immediately. The single worst waste of money in marketing is to continue spending time and money on a promotional piece that isn't working. On the other hand, if your mailer receives higher than 0.20%, you've not only got a success on your hands, but have far exceeded the expectations of any advertising agency.

When your mother told you that first impressions are very important, she was right. This especially holds true for marketing. Consider your primary mailer and the call following an interview. Your customer is interviewing not only the service you offer, but the customer service that comes with it as well. When they call you with questions, the service and information they receive on this first contact will dictate all future business, if any.

E-commerce
& The Internet
▼ ▼ ▼

As more and more arbitrators and mediators are certified and enter the marketplace, the need to set yourself apart from the competition becomes more and more necessary. One of the tools through which you can differentiate yourself from the competition is to provide your prospects an Internet web site detailing you and the services you offer.

A website is relatively inexpensive in comparison to print media that requires graphic design, hard costs, printing fees and postage. And since most people in the US have at least some access to the Internet you can very nearly substitute your brochure and more traditional print media pieces with a well done website. A web site also provides far more space, as well as audio and visual interaction with the viewer. Most web sites for arbitrators and mediators need to include at least some "kitchen" English definition of the ADR processes you provide, the benefits of said processes to your target market (the more detailed the better without getting too wordy), and a printable biography / curriculum vitae / resume, and all available contact information.

The costs involved in establishing a web site include the domain name, the web host, the graphic design or layout, the content, mainte- nance and merchant fees if your site contains an e-commerce package.

The domain name is a category of network on the Internet, or a specific network name. Every Internet address has a suffix that indicates its domain. Some common domain suffixes are .com (com- mercial organizations), .edu (education), .gov (government), and .net (network). You can "buy" a domain name from a variety of sources like Network Solutions (www.NetSol.com) for anywhere from $35.00 US to $120.00 US and for a varying length of time. When choosing a domain name try to find a name that is either the name of your company, like www.Golden-Media.com (the preferred choice), your personal name like www.ArmstrongADR.com, or a generic name like www.ADR.com that identifies your business.

Avoid using words or names that are difficult to spell, difficult to remember, or are spelled incorrectly. You don't want to create any extra barriers between you and your potential clients (and profits). When researching a domain name don't forget to check for domain names that are very similar to yours. You don't want someone else getting your intended business. Another concern – plural vs. singular in a domain name. Again, your strongest position is to "own" a domain that is the same as your business name. If the name of your business is plural (e.g. Resolutions) then try to obtain that name verbatim. If however, there exists a site with a domain name of www.Resolution.com then you may want to either reconsider or submit to the fact that you will have be very diligent and paste the direct link in every piece of email you send (which you should do anyway).

You will also need to find an agent to host your site. Web hosting is the Internet equivalent to the rent you pay a landlord for your storefront. Hosting agents offer a wide variety of packages that include a price breakdown based on the amount of space you are looking to rent, how many mailboxes you need (e.g. Natalie@Golden-Media.com), web site statistics, a catch-all forwarding address, and some even provide full e-commerce shopping packages.

The rates for hosting vary greatly from company to company and are not always in conjunction with the level of service or variety of products they offer. When choosing a hosting agent be wary of the free hosts. They usually make up the lack of service fees you would normally pay by allowing advertisers to place banners on your site. Many of these free sites don't allow the visitor the close out the banner and perhaps more importantly you don't get to choose the type of advertising. You may risk offending your visitors by this kind of blatant and unprofessional commercialism. Something to keep in mind if you're not familiar with Internet hosting or comfortable with the language of the Internet – try to find a host that provides a service representative who can assist you with the process over the phone. You might want to get references or referrals from friends and associates that speak to the host's stability and customer service.

Anyone who is serious about doing business online will need an email address. Email is the main form of communication among cybercitizens or netizens and is the only medium you can use to reach anyone in the online world. Generally speaking your email address will be created when you establish your online account with a host. The address consists of your username followed by the @ sign, your domain name and respective suffix. For example my email address is

Natalie@Golden-Media.com. Natalie is my username, Golden-Media is my domain name, and .com is the suffix. When you sign up for your online account and are at the stage of choosing your user name there are a few things to keep in mind.

Keep your email address simple and easy to spell. The best bet is your first name only or your last name only in addition to your domain name and suffix. In this way you continue to create mindshare with your clients and prospects. You might want to create some administrative addresses like "Subscibe@Golden-Media.com, info@Golden-Media.com, etc. Again, make these addresses as simple and apparent as you can.

Differentiate between your business email address and the email address you utilize for your personal life. You must remain consistent with your business email address and your domain name. This is absolutely critical and the reason is simple; every aspect of your marketing must be consistent to continue to build mindshare within your target market. If you own a domain name (everyone should) to create a more professional appearance, make sure that your business email address matches your domain name. This is easy to do and the benefits are numerous.

Once you have your address you can then create a signature for all of your outgoing email. Not only is attaching a signature to messages standard practice among netizens it can be a powerful marketing tool as well. Your signature is simply an electronic business card. It should contain your name, business name, and your contact information. It could also include your slogan or tag line, mission statement, a link to an Internet map guiding people to your front door, etc.

Below is my signature line:

Natalie J. Armstrong
President

Golden Media "Creative Marketing Solutions"
PO Box 491981
Los Angeles, CA 90049

T: 310-836-4628
F: 520-962-6392
mailto:Natalie@Golden-Media.com
www.Golden-Media.com

My signature also attaches a v-card or virtual business card that when opened goes into detail about Golden Media.

SELLING ON THE NET

Let's get the nasty business of spamming out of the way first. Spamming is the sending of unsolicited messages to people you don't know. Here are ratings of whom customers would be willing to get unsolicited E-mail from:

A company I do business with = 60 %
A magazine I subscribe to = 48%
About my interests and hobbies = 48%
A company I know but haven't done business with − 14%
A company I don't know = 9%
None of the above = 27%

(1001 Ways To Market Your Services, Rick Crandall, PhD, 1998)

The American Marketing Association (AMA) Code of Ethics for Marketing on the Internet is posted on their web site (www.ama.org/about/ama/ethcode.asp). Log on and read it for the complete legal low down. My attitude toward spamming – DON'T DO IT! You will lose more potential clients that could ever have been gained with shady marketing techniques.

On a more positive note – the Internet as a marketing tool does work and it can be extremely lucrative.

Although you still pay for good ideas, good words, good follow-through, and good addresses, you don't have to pay for materials and delivery. With the monetary restriction removed, you can perpetually pummel prospects with propositions. So why shouldn't you?

HOW OFTEN SHOULD YOU CONTACT YOUR PROSPECTS?

How often are they going to be pleased to hear about your offer to help them with their disputes? Is once enough? Is 10 times too many? That all depends on the psychographics of your target market in combination with what you're sending them. For instance if you're sending your target market educational materials or industry updates they will probably be much more flexible on the amount of email they will happily receive from you. If, however, you're sending them blatant advertisements for your services, you will drastically reduce their tolerance for your emails. ResultsLab (www.resultslab.com) says the key to being able to mail frequently, and have it appreciated instead of resented, is to make sure that each mailing is a gift of learning, news, or valuable links. Make sure your mailings are never

sales; and never look like spam; never employ pressure, manipulation, or evasion. These destroy trust and loyalty – an ADR provider's most sought after attributes.

The goal is to get them to think of you often enough, so that when they are actually in need of your service, your practice comes easily to mind as one of the contenders. If you only send one message every six months, your prospect may need your service on the fifth month and not remember to include you in the running. Again, consistency is key to building mindshare with your prospects.

CREATING YOUR OWN EMAIL LIST

Nothing is better than a list of folks you already know. First, they know you. Second, you can start collecting information about them right away and make your message to them much more personal and therefore more meaningful and response evoking.

Call it database marketing, call it customer service, or call it customer relationship management. It's a simple matter of knowing what you can about your customers and then using that knowledge to provide your customers more relevant information (and boost your profits at the same time).

If part of your web site and marketing strategy is to create a regular Internet newsletter or eZine, then you'll want to use your web site to collect at a minimum your visitor's name and email address. You can accomplish this by offering an "opt-in" email form on your web site for your visitors to complete. Collect their data and include them in your future mailings.

COMPOSING YOUR EMAILS

Since email isn't tangible like an envelope or postcard you have to consider what the intangible presence of your email will be. It still represents you and your company to your target market. It is fairly involved and requires you to do your level best to make sure that your message is given its due from the moment is shows up in the recipient's inbox until they decide to act or delete it.

Before we begin with composition of an email there are few tedious details to get through first.

Text vs. HTML

If you have already confirmed that the recipient can read an HTML file then of course HTML with its full color spectrum and graphic capabilities is the preference. If, however, you aren't sure if your database contacts can read an HTML then use text only. It's boring and bland but at least it's readable.

The Header

In a direct mail campaign the envelope is the key. In the Internet world the subject line matters most. You only get one opportunity to make them open your electronic envelope and this is it. As much as I'd love to tell what the perfect header is – it's much easier to tell what to avoid. Avoid meaningless headers like "Important Message" or "Very Important Announcement". Also avoid any vague offers like "Work Smarter, Not Harder" or "Protect Yourself". At all costs avoid the fake familiarity headers like "hi", "Re: how are you doing" these are simply misleading and not appreciated by the recipient.

LET'S TALK WEB SITE STRATEGY

In order to reap the maximum benefits from your web site, you must have a coherent strategy and objective. Strategies and objectives will vary from provider to provider and from site to site. For example, Joe Mediator is interested in collecting feedback information from his visitors to use in future marketing campaigns to help build his caseload, while Joe Arbitrator is mainly focused on selling visitors his newly released ADR book to create additional streams of income via his web site. Both are acceptable objectives, yet each provider can use different strategies to accomplish their objective.

Far too often I've come across web sites that seem to do a better job of confusing the viewer rather than educating them. They simply have zero strategic focus. When the site opens I am bombarded with slow-loading graphics and pop-up windows. There are two sets of navigational buttons that can drive me to any of twenty-plus different pages. Maybe there are unrelated flashy banners at the top of the page and the opening content is simply irrelevant to their services. All fatal mistakes and the result, I leave and go in search of another site that will provide the same service. Which leads me to think how many other visitors did the site drive away for the same reasons and how many potential cases are being lost every single day?

So how can you avoid falling into the same trap? There are several things you can do.

Location, Location, Location

If location is the most important aspect of real estate, then the first page and the first fold of that page (the uppermost part of the page that visitors see first before scrolling down) represent the most valuable real estate on your web site. Simply put, you must utilize this space with the viewer in mind. The first page a viewer sees and the first 30 seconds spent reading that page are the most critical in any visit. In 30 seconds or less a viewer will make a "stay or go" decision and this can make a tremendous difference in being able to fulfill your web site's objective. This is what I call the "30-second rule".

The first fold of your web site must be strategically designed so that in 30 seconds or less, you page clearly communicates the best and most gripping benefit you have to offer your viewers. Fail to do this and you risk loosing potential business. Abide by this cardinal rule, and the results can be simply amazing.

90/10 Content

The content throughout your web site must be created with the visitor in mind. Meaning that 90% of your content should be about the viewer and the remaining 10% should be about your services. Don't bore your visitors with long drawn out mission statements or company philosophies. Instead, create content that's gets right to the point and clearly communicates that you understand your target market and that you are able to provide the solutions they are in need of.

One way this can be accomplished is through the use of creating effective headlines on each page of your web site. Headlines can make or break your web site's success and unfortunately the headline is one of the most frequently overlooked tools by the majority of provider sites. The very first thing that should draw the eyes of your visitors in when they arrive at your web site is a headline that clearly states the biggest benefit that you have to offer. Don't let Graphics, logos, illustrations, menus, links, etc. overpower or distract from this critical element.

Headlines should be located at the very top, center of the page in a larger font size and a color that naturally attracts attention. Use it to show your visitor:

- How you can resolve their pending conflict.

- How you are going to save them time and money while you're doing it.

- How by using your services you'll be helping them with their business, their personal life and even their career.

Let's look at some examples our friend Joe Smith used for his Arbitration and Mediation practice.

1. "Welcome to JoeSmithADR.com"

   Under no circumstance should you ever use your domain name as a title. While it might add to branding your practice, it does not provide a benefit or a reason for visitors to stay on your web site.

2. "Outside The Box"

   You might know what this means and how it applies to you, but I am confident your visitors won't. Who

is this referring to, what does it mean, and why would your visitors understand this? Remember what you are providing. Visitors should not have to read through your entire web site to understand the titles. Make sure that your benefits are clear to everyone instantly.

3. "Stop the Nightmares, Sleep Better"

Don't focus on trying to be clever, instead make sure that your titles are clear to your target market. Be sure your titles are conveying to your visitors why they should be viewing your site. Catchy titles like this can often be much more damaging than amusing.

4. "Alternative Dispute Resolution, for claimants and respondents of new or existing complex litigation"

Huh? Always use kitchen English that your target market is going to understand. Be clear and concise and remember that your web site should be designed with your target market in mind. Your headlines should be straightforward and easy to understand while communicating the benefits of your services to your target market. Don't try and overwhelm visitors with complex phrases or terminology, stick with kitchen English. Follow these simple points and you'll fare just fine.

Navigation: Don't Force Your Visitors to Work, Put Them on Autopilot

The navigational buttons on your web site represent the engine necessary to drive traffic through the site. Like your headlines, the navigational buttons are critical elements of your site and should be created with the end user in mind. They should always be found on the first fold of your site, and when visitors first arrive on your site, they should easily understand that your site is going to be simple to navigate. Don't make your visitors work any more than they have too. Instead, put your viewers on autopilot. Keep it and easy to use and you'll increase the probability of reaching your web site's objective.

Think about it this way, if your visitors are struggling to move around your site, then they are certainly not 100% focused on the benefits you offer or the services you provide. Where do you want their attention to be? Keep their focus in the right location.

Part of creating successful viewer navigation involves selecting the right title and order for your navigational buttons. Remember the theme here is to minimize the amount of effort a visitor is going to have to expend while viewing your site.

Here is a sample of poorly labeled navigational buttons that we might find on our friend Joe Smith's Arbitration and Mediation practice web site.

- ▶ The Future
- ▶ Industry
- ▶ Here's Joe
- ▶ Background
- ▶ Why Joe?

None of these buttons provide value to the site or to the visitor. Meaning that they don't provide a clear understanding of what the visitor will receive from visiting these pages. The majority of web sites make this mistake. It's easy to do, but it's important to fix. Don't make any assumptions about your visitors or their abilities to understand what your buttons mean. Instead, use convincing button names that are clear and easy to understand. This will help to maximize the probability that your visitor's attention is focused on your benefits and services.

More Tips From The Trenches

Once you understand the key elements that should immediately grab your visitors' attention within the first fold of your web site, the elements to avoid become obvious:

NUMBER ONE: AVOID LINKS AND BANNERS THAT DRIVE TRAFFIC AWAY FROM YOUR SERVICES

Be careful not to drive traffic away from your web site with distracting banners and links. While there are a few situations that warrant placing a banner at the top of your homepage (i.e. you're promoting something specific or you want to grab your visitors' attention) you need to make sure you're not driving your traffic right into the hands of your competition.

I've seen a number of provider sites who place links like Amazon.com, Yahoo shopping, or even other search engines on their site. When I've inquired about the links the usual answer has something to do with obtaining "click-through" credits for sales made by visitors who have passed or clicked through their site.

Affiliate programs are a great idea, but if you compare the potential amount of income earned from driving sales for Amazon.com or Yahoo via click-throughs versus the amount of income that could be realized from keeping viewers focused on your site and service benefits and ultimately receiving one or two additional cases, you'll quickly see there's hardly a comparison. You work so hard to bring traffic to your site, why open the back door for your visitors before they even step inside? Think carefully before placing any links or banners within the first fold of your web site; this is the most valuable piece of real estate on your site don't give it away.

Number Two: Avoid Distracting Graphics and Animation

Words sell, not graphics. So if visitors spend the first 30 seconds at your site trying to figure out how to make your long Flash presentation stop, or waiting for large graphics to load, you can be sure that they're not going to stick around to read more. While there is a time and place for graphics and animation, be certain that if you've chosen to include any on your site, you've done so to strategically enhance your message and further illustrate your service benefits, not for your own self-gratification.

Number Three: Avoid "About You" Text Such As Mission Statements

Sites that seem intent on boring you to death with long, elaborate pages that talk about company goals and mission statements violate the 90/10 rule. Think about it, a mission statement is about what your company wants to achieve, not about how your visitors are going to benefit from doing business with you. While there may be some cases of these benefits being implied in mission statements, the fact is you are asking your visitors to work harder to learn these benefits. Don't. Keep it simple and keep it about your target market. I do believe mission statements can be a valuable guide for companies to follow; so, if you are adamant about posting your mission statement on your web site, don't use your valuable real estate to do so. Instead, dedicate a separate button and page solely for that purpose.

Bread & Butter Strategies for Mediators and Arbitrators

YOU MUST ESTABLISH YOUR CREDIBILITY

When a provider promotes their services online, they are typically selling the end user on a relationship with themselves. This requires that you spend more time and effort establishing your credibility and developing a rapport with your visitors than is typically required on a site selling a physical product. When selling conflict resolution as a service, you, the provider become the product. So establishing your credibility is essentially establishing your value as an arbitrator or mediator. This is absolutely critical in persuading your end users to select your services over your competition.

You need to not only establish the benefits of the resolution services that you're offering; you need to establish the value of your firm resolving the dispute.

There are a few different ways you can accomplish this:

1. **Include a good, professional photograph of your-self.** Give your visitors a professional image to associate you with. It will go a long way to establishing your credibility with your target market. It may even prove to be the deciding factor in your services being selected for that case.

2. **In addition to your C/V Resume Bio, provide testimonials from previous clients about your services.** Few things will speak louder for you than the testimonials of previously satisfied clients. Use them for everything they are worth. You can retype them on your site or even better you can have your web designer scan in the actual letter you received (erasing case information) and post it on your web site. Testimonials from previous clients will do two things. First, they will translate into benefits that prospective clients can relate to and second; testimonials will provide evidence that other clients have been pleased with your work.

Be Sure Your Content Is Specific About Your Practice

Previously we talked about the importance of specializing your area of practice. Be certain that your web site content follows suit. Providing information alone about what you've done for other clients won't motivate visitors to make the connection and visualize what you'll be able to do to help them settle their dispute. You must be absolutely specific about what you are exactly offering your visitors. I suggest you spend some time reviewing other providers in your market segment and compare services. Do you offer the same exact type of services? What makes you different from your competitors?

One of the most influential aspects of your web site will be providing visitors with enough information about the services you provide. Don't violate the 90/10 rule, but do be sure to educate your viewers about your practice. Otherwise, they might not be able to make an informed decision.

Make It Easy for Visitors to Contact You

I don't think I can stress this enough. Make it as easy a process as possible for your visitors to contact you. One of the single most dangerous mistakes you can make is to force your visitors to work harder to find your contact information. Don't let them loose focus on the reason why they chose to visit your site in the first place. Keep all of your contact information in a bold, static location on every page. If you're utilizing a "Contact Us" page that contains a web form to collect data from visitors, that's fine, just make sure that a visitor can reach that page from any location on your web site within one click.

Think of it this way; you've worked long and hard to build your web site and you've worked even longer and harder to bring that visitor in for a look around. You have educated them on the benefits you offer, and you've motivated them to take one more step to contacting you. Don't make them click the back button 50 times to reach your home page to find your email address or phone number. Make it easy for your visitors to contact you!

Network & List Your Site In Local Directories

You are selling a service, therefore the location of your clients is going to be important. So while almost all of the traffic techniques used to drive visitors to product-based sites can be applied to conflict resolution based sites, I would like to mention a few techniques that you can use to boost "local" traffic.

First, if you're not doing so already, be sure to network with other local target market associations and organizations. If you want local traffic, start making personal connections with your target market within a 30-mile radius of your office. Be creative and look for networking opportunities for you and your web site. Consider sponsoring an e-Zine that is disseminated to a local chapter of your target market's associations and organizations.

Second; list you site in local online directories. The plain truth is that local online directories can be a fantastic source of traffic. There are plenty of local online directories that list only two or three businesses in categories that should be quite popular with your target market. Consumers are becoming more comfortable searching for information online; convert these local directories to local referral services.

Encourage Referrals & Repeat Clients

Always, always, always follow up with existing clients. Remember there are only three ways to grow your practice.

1. Increase the number of new clients

2. Increase your fees

3. Increase the frequency a client returns for your services

If your clients are truly satisfied with the service you provided them is there any reason why they shouldn't return to work with you again? Don't forget about your Communication Plan™. Be sure to touch every previous client in addition to your prospects. Just because you've serviced their needs before, doesn't necessarily mean that your mindshare will continue to hold. Following up with them can be as simple as a phone call or an email and the results can be tremendous for your practice. Furthermore I would be willing to bet that a solid majority of your previous clients know a number of people who would benefit from your services. So don't be afraid to remind previous clients that you're out there, and don't be afraid to ask for referrals. If you've done a good job for someone, they'll likely be more than happy to refer their friends and business associates to you. But if you don't ask, they'll rarely think to do it! Don't leave this to chance.

Summary

The first fold of your website is the most valuable real estate on your entire site. Make sure you have a solid strategy for this section. Follow the rules and be certain that your web site is designed with your target market viewer in mind. Avoid slow loading fancy graphics and work to increase the average length of a visitor's stay.

I get a lot of e-mail from people who think that selling ADR services over the Web must require an entirely different approach than selling a product. They think they will need to use an entirely different set of tools and techniques, that their web site design must be noticeably different, and that to drive visitors to their sites they'll need to use some new, cutting edge strategies.

My experience has shown this simply isn't true.

The only real difference between selling conflict resolution services versus tennis racquets over the Internet is the focus of your content. When you sell a physical product, every aspect of your site design and sales copy focuses on how the product is going to solve visitors' needs and benefit them. When you sell conflict resolution services over the Internet, the focus of your content is on how you are going to solve visitors' needs and benefit them. So long as your content follows the 90/10 rule, you should be fine.

WEB SITE EVALUATION WORKSHEET

Whether you have an existing web site or you are thinking about establishing an Internet presence, start by evaluating each page on your site and be able to answer the following questions. Remember each page must serve a purpose.

1. What is the primary objective of my web site?

2. Am I fulfilling this objective? If not, why?

3. Is my web site strategy appropriate for reaching my objective?

4. Is my site easily navigated? Are my visitors on autopilot?

5. Are my pages in the proper order and are the properly labeled?

6. What function does each page serve?

7. What value does each page and its content add (or subtract) from the site and the visitor's experience?

8. What is the traffic flow and where do I want visitors to go after they have viewed each page?

9. Are the colors and images utilized target market appropriate?

10. Is my contact information easily located? And finally…

11. Is my web site programmed to load quickly and efficiently?

Customer Service

▼ ▼ ▼

"Eighty percent of your results come from twenty percent of your efforts."
Paraphrased from Vilfredo Pareto

How is it that some providers seem able to convene more cases than others? Are they better at what they do? Well maybe, but more than likely they approach each prospect with a philosophy of service that lends itself to creating relationships more than revenue. They focus on "you" not "me". This is an approach that anyone and everyone can apply. This simple approach is the key to what I believe is the most powerful business (and life) strategy you can employ.

Once you begin to use it you will always stand out in the minds, hearts, and checkbooks of your clients, friends, colleagues, and family. If you can master the mantra of "Serve before you sell", success will follow.

I'd like to make an important distinction by considering the definitions of 'customer' and 'client'.

Customer: A person who purchases a commodity or service.
Client: A person who is under the protection of another.

Using the word customer is fine as long you always think of your customers like clients. You must serve before you sell. This is the magic bullet in marketing. Serve before you sell.

What does "a person who is under the protection of another" mean? It means that you don't sell them a service so that you can make the largest one-time profit possible. You must understand and appreciate what they need when they need it. Frequently in our business, this means understanding what the client often cannot articulate. Once you have identified what they need and provide it, your clients become loyal sources of referrals.

When a divorcing couple comes to you looking for assistance with a child-custody case what are they really looking for? Someone to draw a visitation and support contract? No they are in all likelihood looking to you to assist them in coming to an amicable and reasonable agreement that will ultimately let them dissolve their married relationship, retain a co-parent relationship, and jointly allow them both to continue as positive role models and powerful influences in the lives of their children. They want to sleep at night knowing that they have crafted the best possible agreement they could. They are buying the hope of resolution and peace.

Whatever you do, if you focus on giving value instead of manipulating and maneuvering, you win over many more prospects, clients, colleagues and friends. And you will be rewarded in ways you never dreamed.

Instead of asking yourself, "What do I have to say to get people to buy my service"? Ask yourself, "What do I have to give? What benefit can I offer?"

The more value you give your clients, the more value you generate.

This may seem very obvious to you. But I'm always amazed that this basic concept eludes most providers. Think about our industry. What do our services provide? Solutions! We are selling solutions to problems. We are resolutionists. Reflect this in your marketing, in your communications, and in your customer service. Remember to sell your clients what they need versus what you have to sell.

Think about the different people with whom you deal each day. Think about them one at a time. Think about each one as a client. Focus on what that person's real needs in dealing with you are. What results are they after? What is your role in this transaction? What is the impact of the transaction? What does dealing with you provide them?

Test this.

Choose one prospect that you would like to convert into client. Let your new understanding of service work for them and you. With sincerity and enthusiasm connect with them via e-mail, personal letter, or one-on-one meeting with respect and loyalty. Serve them before you sell them and you'll begin to see the dramatic difference it make in the way they respond to you.

Networking

"It's not whom you know but how you are known to them."
Theodore Levitt

Most mediators and arbitrators (most business people for that matter) are aware that one of the keys to a successful business is networking. Making the acquaintance of someone who is a potential client or a potential source of referrals can be one of the greatest investments we make in business.

As powerful as this particular tool can be, it takes some forethought. For instance, most of us belong to any number of ADR associations and organizations. These groups are usually a never-ending stream of information and camaraderie. They are, however, for our own edification and not always the most effective networking locales. Choose instead to network in the associations and organizations that support your target market. If you want to hear more construction disputes, join the associations that general contractors and design professionals belong to. If you want to hear employment disputes, join the human resource groups. You get the idea.

Offer to speak to their member base on the benefits of ADR to their industry, provide educational seminars, etc. Get involved with your potential clients and let them see your professionalism, your communication skills, and your innate understanding of their industry. Let them know that you understand them, can empathize with them and freely speak their language. In this way, you become an authority in ADR for the their profession.

The tricky part — not waiving your neutrality. Be careful that your new acquaintances do not get the impression that you would turn cases in their favor based on a common membership or on an inappropriate and misunderstood "obligation to acquaintances." Wear your standards and ethics on your sleeve, let potential clients know about the rules of disclaimer, and that if put in an uncomfortable and unethical situation, you will stand down as the provider and make a referral to another competent ADR service provider.

Our ethics and standards of conduct as an industry are one of a few uniting fronts ADR providers should get behind and use as a fabulous, powerful marketing tool (the enclosed CD contains the majority of the rules of conduct and codes of ethics in North America).

Networking is ideal for anyone who finds it easier to sell someone else than to sell themselves, because when done effectively the more you promote others with whom you're networking, the more likely they are to promote you.

We've found networking to be the most popular way for arbitrators and mediators to start to build or to maintain a practice. Networking gives you a chance to convey your interest in a prospect's needs and concerns, as well as relaying your specific knowledge about the prospect's industry. It gives you the opportunity to find out what they need and show them how your practice can serve them better.

Networking also provides your prospects a chance to determine whether or not they like you. Almost everyone likes to do business with someone they like, especially in a service industry like conflict resolution.

On the other hand, even for those arbitrators and mediators who happen to like the personalized approach of selling their services through networking, it is one of the most time-consuming marketing activities. Generally speaking, the one-time, press-the-flesh contact doesn't work. More often, networking is a long-term marketing strategy. You may however, be lucky enough to make a contact at anytime at any event that will lead directly to business. Usually though, in order to get business through networking, you need to spend time and energy week after week and month after month building relationships.

The idea behind networking is for your prospects to get to know you well enough to establish some visibility with your prospects which will lead to familiarity which will in turn lead to credibility – that elusive asset is what makes people want to hire you.

Networking, either in person or electronically, is one of the most certain means for making sure you are in the right place at the right time. It's simple math really, the more people you meet, the more likely you are to find people to do business with. The more you keep in touch with the people you know, the more likely they will turn into customers and clients. This is the primary advantage of networking your way to more business.

And there's the rub.

How can a mediator or arbitrator create a relationship that is deep enough for someone to trust with his or her case, but not so personal that relationship is imbued with bias?

Networking is the answer.

Since networking is time consumptive, you'll want to be sure to spend your networking investment where you're most likely to get a high rate of return. Many service providers think that the more they network, the more business they'll get. Eventually all their efforts will pay off, but there's a better way.

The key to make networking pay off is to make sure that you're networking in the right places. You want to carefully choose your opportunities to include those events at which you're almost certain to encounter the very people who need and are interested in your practice specialty.

Make sure to join associations and organizations whose members are either potential clients or who will become a source of referrals. Belonging to any of the hundreds of conflict resolution associations is great – but not the best place to find customers. Alternative Dispute Resolution (ADR) associations are intended to provide you edification about the conflict resolution industry. You want to circulate just as

10 Tips for One-On-One Networking

1. Arrive at meetings and group activities at least fifteen minutes early.

2. Stop waiting for something to happen to you – take the initiative.

3. Always speak with confidence and a smile.

4. Carry a large supply of business cards.

5. Make sure you get a business card from the people you meet.

6. Have a pen or pencil handy to make notes on the cards of your contacts for follow-up information.

7. Concentrate on the one person to whom are speaking – don't be guilty of roving eyes.

8. Stay at least fifteen minutes after the event to exchange cards etc.

9. Follow-up *immediately* with anyone who expressed an interest in your service.

10. Always send a thank-you note or place a phone call of thanks to anyone who sends you business.

much, if not more, in the associations to which your target market belongs.

Networking requires too much time and energy to join organizations that only peripherally address your market. If your practice specialty is construction then you will want to join your local construction law associations as well as some of the design professionals' organizations.

Their meetings, seminars and conferences provide golden opportunities for introductions and connections. Even if an event provides no new business immediately it will probably provide information that will be helpful in obtaining business and better serving your clients.

Now, just being listed as a member of an organization or showing up at the annual dinner isn't enough. Success through networking requires repeated interaction to build a connection.

Many people who are just starting out may consider this kind of marketing frivolous socializing. But when you think about it most of our business process is social in nature. Also ... if you've joined the right organizations then there is nothing frivolous about your networking activities. The costs involved are business expenses and are tax deductible if you've kept proper records.

Even for those providers who have plenty of business you are best advised to remain active in at least one group since generating business takes time – you don't want to wait to start networking when you need business right away. And since out of sight is out of mind you need to be around when someone with whom you spoke a year ago suddenly needs your service. If you're not around and someone else is … guess who will get the business you've worked so hard for?

When an event presents itself get ready to do business. Dress as you would for any business meeting and stock your wallet with business cards. Once you arrive don't just stand around with your hands in your pockets or hover around the appetizer table – take the initiative to meet new people.

Be careful not to fall into the rut of talking only to those who already know and like you. Don't latch onto one person and spend all your time on him or her - circulate. Make a point of connecting with a few new people at each meeting. The more people you meet the more people you can build business relationships with.

That said, don't slight the people with whom you've worked so hard to establish a rapport. A balance of reconnecting with people you've met before and meeting new people is the key. Acting as the organization's greeter or chairing the membership committee is a perfect position for meeting all the attendees and a great way to overcome any networking shyness.

Becoming an active member is one of the best ways to build relationships. You can make contacts by attending meetings or sitting in on chat sessions, but getting involved in goal-directed activities builds relationships that can develop into business.

So participate in the organization you join, serve on a committee, lead a community project or fund-raising event. You'll earn the respect and trust from the other members (your target market) which is imperative to gaining their business.

Once you've made a promising contact, don't monopolize his or her time in an in-depth conversation. Save these longer conversations for follow-up contacts. Follow-up via phone, personal note, e-mail or meeting to find out how you can help them. Take the time to ask them questions, and listen to find out more about their concerns and needs.

> ** Note: this approach is only for those contacts who will refer you to their clients (e.g. attorneys or behaviorists) and is not appropriate if you're dealing with one of the parties directly.

Remember that one of the best ways to get business is to refer business. This may be the most important tip of successful networking. People tend to refer business to those who refer business to them. Keep notes on the services your contacts are looking for and provide them a *confident* referral.

The more you give, the more you'll get!

Speaking
▼ ▼ ▼

"The door to success is always marked 'Push'."
American Proverb

Marketing an ADR practice requires a well-rounded marketing menu.
It's necessary to use a variety of tools from the marketing shed in
order to construct a solid practice. One of the tools most used by
mediators and arbitrators is speaking engagements and/or educational
seminars. This is a great method to make yourself known as an
authority in your target market's industry.

One powerful method of marketing is public speaking. For those of
you who are comfortable with presenting information or motivational
speeches to an audience, you can easily establish yourself as an
authority in our industry as well as an authority in your target
market's industry. For those of you who barely escape getting hives
at the mere thought of public speaking, you might want to consider a
partnership with someone who is an experienced and professional
speaker. The benefits to speaking directly to your target market are
multifold. You put yourself forward as an authority in both your own
industry and your target market's, you more easily create a relation-

ship with a potential client, and you receive invaluable feedback about your target market's goals, preferences, and aspirations in choosing a provider.

So speak up, speak out, and let your prospects hear and meet you.

Below are some timeline tips if you're handling the promotion yourself.

1. Check the industry's calendar for their monthly and annual meetings. Either become involved in the association's event or schedule your own so that it does not conflict with theirs. Most organizations require six months to a year advance notice for annual conferences and a couple of weeks to a year for monthly meetings. Choose a date that is a minimum of 90 days away, but preferably in excess of 120 days.

2. Choose a date that provides you enough time to create a database or arrange for use of the association's newsletter and member database. Give this section of preparation your best timeline guess, and then double that amount of time.

3. Set aside enough time (and money) to create your Web site or print media (including any handouts), and address and apply postage. Double the expected time for creation and production to allow safety net for yourself.

4. For events that require participants to travel or make overnight accommodations (especially for multiple-day events), you should give them 90 to 180 days advance notice. For events that are designed for a local group, or if the event will consume a single day, four to eight weeks' notice is sufficient.

Focus on the needs of your audience, and your audience will focus on you.

When you are putting an idea together for a speaking engagement there is one factor you must not overlook, the topic. It's easy to choose a topic. Simply ask. Whether you ask your audience on the phone, in person or by means of a written questionnaire, the answers to the following two questions will become the basis for your speech.

First: What three things would you most like to see covered in this speech?

Second: If you could have only one of these covered, which would it be?

Once you've determined your topic you need to plan out your content. Audiences tune out self-promotion instantly and it's very difficult to win them back. Save that for the private question and answer session after your speech as been delivered. Instead, your content should provide beneficial information to the audience.

RULES OF THE ROAD FOR SPEAKERS

Opening

1. Begin on time. Don't penalize the folks who arrived on time by waiting for latecomers. You will only antagonize the listeners who are on time and the latecomers won't appreciate you generosity.

2. Start with lots of energy. Show enthusiasm for your topic in your delivery style. Your opening will set the tone for the entire encounter.

3. Thoroughly prepare your opening.

Body

1. Introduction: Whether someone else introduces you or you introduce yourself, make it brief, but make sure that your audience knows you are qualified to speak on the topic at hand.

2. Opening remarks: Again, make it brief and keep it light. Let your audience know that you are glad to be speaking to them, that you are happy that they have attended, and that you truly care about them and the topic.

3. Introduction: If there are fewer than about 20 people in attendance, you can ask them to introduce them-selves if they are not already a close-knit group.

4. Needs and concerns: By asking your audience about their concerns and needs you are letting them know that you care about them and will customize your presentation to address their specific issues. Again, if the group is small enough, you can ask them to address their issues as they introduce themselves. Be sure that you list each concern on a flip chart or marker board so that the audience can see that you have addressed each one.

5. Details: These are the mundane things you may or may not need to mention prior to the substantive portion of your speech. The location of the bathrooms, rules about smoking, location of telephones, break times, lunch information etc.

6. Lecture: Most lectures are less than fun. In fact the word itself conjures up negative childhood memories for most of us. To keep your audience awake and engaged encourage questions throughout. Be careful not to allow your audience to sidetrack to far though.

7. Participatory exercises: Use participatory exercises if they are appropriate. Your audience will come alive with each one and you'll give them an opportunity to get actively involved in the learning process.

8. Breaks: If your speaking engagement lasts longer than 2 hours, provide participants a break of 10 or 15

minutes. Encourage them to stand up and stretch their legs. Announce the amount of time you'll give them, then stick to it.

Closing

1. Summarize your key points: Review the highlights of what you just told them.

2. Acknowledge sponsors or assistants: If your program was sponsored – thank them. Likewise, acknowledge any assistants and express your gratitude.

3. Thank the participants: Without an audience, there would be no speech. Let them know how much you appreciate their attentiveness.

4. Call for action: Challenge your audience to apply the information you provided them, to continue their research or education, or take whatever step might be appropriate.

5. Close with flair: Leave the audience feeling positive about the experience and the information you shared. Use humor, quotes, anecdotes or basically anything that will make your audience feel good.

6. Plan and rehearse your closing: Your closing should be well thought out and rehearsed. Don't wing it. Often it is the last thing you said that will stick in

their minds the most. A big, positive finish is very important.

7. End on time: Remember that participants have arranged their schedules around the announced start and finish times. Be courteous at all costs.

Publishing ▼ ▶ ▼

PROMOTING YOUR ADR PRACTICE THROUGH NEWSLETTERS AND E-ZINES

Let's first concede that most readers are in actuality skimmers. They skim through the material looking for immediate information gratification. So to accommodate all the skimmers I'll skip right to good stuff.

Selling through newsletters and e-zines (electronic or e-mail magazines) can be summed up with NEWS.

> **N = Name**: Telling people who you are, where to find you and what you provide
>
> **E= Enticement**: Drawing people to your publication by showing that you can provide what your prospects want and that you're an expert.
>
> **W= Written Words**: Giving specific features and reasons why your prospects should choose your

product, service or cause over those of your competitors.

S= Sell: Telling readers what action to take – return the reply card, call the toll-free number, or enroll in a training seminar.

Newsletters and e-zine have an advantage over other direct mail pieces or email messages. They aren't considered junk mail. Instead they're happy, helpful, brief pieces of targeted information.

They promote specific goals and provide a service while selling a service. In general, newsletters and e-zines are a good way to bring in new prospects, keep in touch with existing clients, ad value to your services, reinforce your specialty, establish expertise and credibility, spur word-of-mouth referrals, inform and educate, bring back lost clients, publicize your practice, and network within your target market.

"A newsletter should be long enough to say what you need to say and short enough to be read on the way to the wastebasket."
-Mark Beach

To achieve these goals, however, your material must be read. Newsletters and e-zines that get read contain useful information presented in appropriate and appealing ways. Successful promotional newsletters and e-zines get people to read not only what interests them, but also what you want them to read.

The Tried & True Do's & Don'ts

At newsletter seminars throughout the world, people mention the same items that they like and don't like to see in newsletters.

People like:
- ▶ Interesting subjects
- ▶ Short articles
- ▶ Good visuals
- ▶ Easy-to-skim designs
- ▶ Bulleted lists
- ▶ Content telling how to make money, save time
- ▶ Clear organization
- ▶ Calendars
- ▶ Offers, benefits

People Don't Like:
- ▶ Intimidating pages
- ▶ Disorganized information
- ▶ Long, continuing articles
- ▶ Overly frequent mailings
- ▶ Irrelevant content
- ▶ Impersonal tone
- ▶ Receiving multiple copies
- ▶ Chaotic page design
- ▶ Too many pages

Elaine Floyd "Marketing with Newsletters"

Readers are attracted to by content and design that's targeted to their interests. For instance, print your non-profit organization's newsletter on inexpensive paper to show them that you spend hard-won money frugally. If you're in private practice print your newsletter on crisp, heavy stock to make a more impressive statement.

Now, how do you go about finding pertinent information and advice to provide your readers?

Some types of newsletter content are news and articles, success stories, customer profiles, survey results, helpful information or opinions & editorials. For news article you might write about current legislation as it applies to your target market, a recent event, a new product or service or calendared event. Success stories and anecdotes (remember to be careful about the confidentiality rules) are an easy way to "show" your prospects the benefits of using your service. Profiles about your clients are a great way to create client loyalty. You can keep your client's attention by giving them yours. You might also want to provide your readers with survey responses that promote ADR or your practice in specific (testimonials work just as well for this category of content). And finally, helpful information is what it's all about. Remember that to transform a prospect into a client, you must serve them before you sell to them.

Frequencies … publish your newsletter at least quarterly and prefer-ably bi-monthly or monthly. If you feel unable to make a commitment to regular publication, admit it. One bookstore even calls its newslet-ter "The Occasional."

Does haphazardness in your publication schedule show a lack of commitment to your readers? Will an irregularly published newsletter hurt rather than help your image? I've never known anyone to be hurt by publishing just one promotional newsletter. The disadvantage is that they didn't stick with the project long enough to reap the benefits of longevity, but they did get the attention of some of their prospects. Every issue builds on the efforts of the last newsletter. Within reason, the more issues your prospects see the greater the promotional effects.

Print Media ▼ ▼ ▼

"To be persuasive, we must be believable. To be believable, we must be credible. To be credible, we must be truthful."
Edward R. Murrow

NEWSLETTER TIPS

Newsletters are a powerful resource in marketing. They are used to educate, inform and market to nearly any and all geographically specific, industry specific, or interest specific groups. Newsletters are a low-cost and effective method to constantly remind potential customers of your name and business. According to Howard Penn Hudson, the president of The Newsletter Clearinghouse, newsletters are so effective because they are targeted.

Some Import Newsletter Tips:

1. Fill you newsletter with interesting information – brief points that your readers will find useful.

2. Proofread your content carefully. Remember that your media is a direct reflection of you and your service.

3. Be informative. Educate you readers on news in the industry, and cover a wide variety of topics.

4. Be brief. You don't need to create the New York Times each volume. Your readers are looking for a "quick fix" of information from you about their industry and your service.

5. Make sure that you follow through on the promised delivery schedule. Publish at least quarterly – bimonthly or even monthly are the best.

6. Keep your customers at the top of the topic list. Use testimonials. What others have to say about you and your service goes much farther than anything you could say about yourself.

7. Have a specific goal in mind when you create your newsletter. If you are confused about what its purpose is, your audience will be, too.

If you have specific questions about how to create a newsletter for your marketing campaign, or how to build and distribute to a targeted audience, give us call for a free consultation.

A PICTURE IS WORTH MORE THAN YOU THINK

People love to look at photographs. They are magnets. No matter where they appear on a page, they attract the reader's eye. Research shows that the best-read parts of the newspaper are the small print captions under the pictures.

That's worth repeating.

Captions under photographs are the best-read words.

Pictures rivet a reader's attention while they read the copy underneath. You can put a lot of information in a four- or five-line caption. Don't make the mistake of making captions too long or you will lose the powerful effect.

Using photographs in your brochures and on your website as well as your c.v. / resume allow your potential clients to "get to know you" without you having to be present. Just think how uncomfortable you are when waiting for someone who is a stranger to you versus someone you've previously met or seen. A photograph allows people to make a visual connection to you without a physical introduction, and consequently increases their comfort with you.

A note on portraits – it isn't necessary to sit in front of a blue or gray backdrop to make an impression. In fact, think about having your portrait taken in a library, park, office setting, etc. Think also about how the photograph will fit into the overall color scheme of your media, as well as the "personality" of your collateral pieces.

WHAT PEOPLE SAY ABOUT YOU!

Trust. It's why people hire you. But it takes a lot of time and money to persuade a prospect to trust you enough to give you his business. The best way to generate trust is obvious, but it isn't used very much: Testimonials. That's why I recommend using testimonials at every opportunity. They're free, relatively easy to get, and flexible enough to add potency to almost any marketing campaign. Best of all, they're believed.

The primary reason that people don't buy from you is not price, location, or service (though to continue in business for any length of time, these elements must be present in spades). No, it's usually trust. Trust is the critical element in closing the sale. That's where testimonials can be put into action. Prospective clients are far more likely to trust what others have to say about your service than what you have to say about yourself.

It's easy to do. Testimonials can be compiled by sending out a simple survey in which you ask your clients to rate your service, speed, cost, and so on. Invite them to make comments on their letterhead, letting them know that their comments will be used in your marketing. THIS DISCLOSURE IS IMPERATIVE FOR OUR INDUSTRY AND ITS CODES OF CONFIDENTIALITY.

Once you have one testimonial or a hundred, put them to work for you.

> ▸ Print a booklet of your best testimonials (the thicker,

the better), and send them to your customers, prospects, and the media.

▶ Use testimonials in your print ads.

▶ Devote at least one panel in your brochure to testimonials from customers.

▶ Put testimonials on the walls of your conference or meeting area, or on a wall where your customers can see them.

TIPS FOR NEWSPAPER AND PERIODICAL ADVERTISING

The Golden Rule: Repitition

Design and copywriting are crucial to the success of your advertising, but always remember that repetition is the key. For every three advertisements viewed, the average consumer will ignore two. It takes an average consumer nine exposures to an ad before the ad is readily remembered. Thus, a specific ad should be run AT LEAST 27 TIMES in media directed toward a specific consumer niche before the ad is changed.

Design   Tips

1. Don't underestimate the importance of your ad's appearance. Far more people will see your ad than you or your place of business, so their opinion of your business will be shaped by your ad. Don't let

the newspaper people design your ad, and don't let them write the copy. If they do, it will end up looking and sounding like all the other ads in the paper. Your competition is not just other providers, but everybody who advertises.

2. Make sure you have a strong headline – if you don't get their attention with the headline, neither will the rest of the ad.

3. Put a border around your ad.

4. Use testimonials.

5. Don't change an ad that is working. As tired as you, your friends and family may become of seeing the same ad week after week, "if it ain't broke, don't fix it". Repetition and reinforcement are the keys to successful newspaper advertising.

Writing Content

▼ ▼ ▼

The key to effectively communicating with potential clients is the same key many mediators and arbitrators utilize in their practice and offer their clients as advice: Clarity and Brevity. Simply say what you mean in a succinct fashion. People will respond to this technique of clarity and brevity if you are tactful and truthful.

Just say it! Be clear and be brief.

THE WORDS YOU CHOOSE

Quick Tips: When writing content for any promotional piece, remember to use words that …

> ▶ Have a Benefit Orientation
> ▶ Are Positive
> ▶ Are Active as Opposed to Passive
> ▶ Are Clear
> ▶ Are Brief
> ▶ Have a Visceral Effect

For a list of Words that Sell see the Appendix for my favorites.

Writing copy (or content) is all about persuading and motivating your reader. In order to persuade and motivate your reader, you will need to break the process of writing into two sections – the first is prior to writing and the second is while you're writing.

Prior to writing, you need to analyze your service. First, analyze your practice from both your perspective and your potential client's. Find those qualities about your service that you think will be of greatest interest to your target market. Second, think about your position in the market place. How and why is your practice and service superior to the competition? Third, what are the tastes of your readers? Are they executives, teenagers, housewives, etc.? Alter the "tone" of your message depending on the personality of the reader. And fourth, does the copy you have in mind fit with your entire marketing concept?

While you're writing it's imperative not to lose sight of the objective: to sell your service. Remember to use words that persuade and motivate. Write to sell.

Here are seven things to keep in mind while writing:

1. Don't overstate with too many words like fabulous and extraordinary. They will destroy your credibility.

2. Be accurate and truthful.

3. Be specific. Vague approximations leave the reader unsatisfied.

4. Be organized. Your message should progress logically from headline to clincher.

5. Write for easy reading. The style should suit your reader, but some rules apply to all content writing. Seek to write smooth, uncluttered, involving and persuasive content.

6. Don't offend the reader. Be careful when using humor.

7. Revise and edit, revise and edit, revise and edit.

WRITING FOR BROCHURES AND WEBSITES

If you want a brochure or website to promote your practice then there are a few guidelines to keep in mind when sitting down to begin the creative process. First you need to establish some clear goals for your media. What will the primary use be? The most common are:

▸ To act as a catalyst or call to action for potential clients
▸ To act as a reference for your services
▸ To support other marketing activities

Most small practices or firms will employ a brochure or website which will of course need content. Make a list of what you want to convey to prospects. What service will you include? What biographical information will you provide? Do you have illustrations to use? Can you list testimonials and endorsements? These are the facts section of your brochure or website.

Your next list should include the primary concerns and issues your readers will have about the service you offer. For instance, if your practice specializes in construction arbitration, a main concern for potential clients will be whether or not you have a specific and extensive background in the construction industry. Readers want to know if you can "speak their language" and read their specialized reports and blueprints fluently.

Other examples of potential issues are what the costs will be, how long will the process take, is the process formal or informal, does the reader need an attorney or not, how can they engage the other party, etc. Whatever you identify as the readers' main concerns should be addressed in your content. I happen to think that a good rule of thumb for this section is that it should consume more than half of the brochure's or website's space. You want to make sure that the reader understands that *your* practice understands the reader.

The concerns and issues that the majority of your readers will need to have addressed should be listed in subheads that create the main copy on the inside panels. And the facts about your services and the processes you offer should be organized in the copy with their respective illustrations.

The same holds true for a website. The opening page should contain your logo or illustration and a short, clear description of your practice and its target market. When you create your website content a rule of 90 – 10 is best. 90% of the site should be about the reader and their issues and concerns being met and managed and 10% of the site should be about you, the provider.

If you're not clear on the content or its reason for existence – the reader won't be either and you've just wasted your efforts on something that won't stand a chance at reaching its marketing goals.

Tips and Treasures
▼ ▼ ▼

1. Know Your Audience – For instance, if you're a divorce mediator you might consider a divorcing couple your clients … But your marketing audience is probably counselors, therapists, clergy etc. Target your marketing toward your referral base and look for an increase in response rates.

2. Hard Luck Harvesting – When a competitor goes out of business you can turn their misfortune into money. Advertising in the Yellow Pages is always a great way to reach customers and for pennies on the dollar your local Yellow Pages will forward calls that your now defunct competitor would have received.

3. "Goodwill is the only asset that competition cannot undersell or destroy." Marshall Field, Businessman and philanthropist.

4. "People expect a certain reaction from a business, and when you pleasantly exceed those expectations,

you've somehow passed an important psychological threshold." Richard Thalheimer, President, The Sharper Image.

5. Positively Post Script – Most people use a P.S. in their letter as an afterthought. But Siegfried Vogele, a professor of direct marketing in Munich, Germany, would recommend otherwise. He has done extensive eye tests to determine where people look on a mailing piece. First, they look to see who sent it, then at how the letter is addressed; then their eye jumps to the signature. The next thing they read is the P.S. So use a P.S. in every piece to motivate, reinforce, emphasize, or introduce.

6. Direct Mail Magic – Most people sort their mail according to clues the packaging provides them. We put items of like size together, then items of like content together (like bills). Items sent priority mail, checks, and pieces that look like personal correspondence (birthday cards, invitations etc.) are opened first and always. You can take advantage of this natural tendency by printing a "teaser" on the envelope such as "Five ways to reduce stress in the workplace". Blind mailing (a plain envelope with a small return address that does not reveal the business name) also works well. A personalized piece of mail works much better than "Manager" or " Occupant". Use a real stamp as opposed to mail indicia or bulk rate insignia and send you mailings in closed enve-

lopes as opposed to the window envelopes in which most people receive their bills.

7. The Pen is Mightier than the Label – Spending the time and effort to hand address your direct mail envelopes can reap a rate of opening of 45% (as opposed to the usual 1 or 2 percent).

8. Secrets of the Spreadsheet – Instead of spending more money on your marketing, stop and analyze the money you're currently spending. Create a simple spreadsheet that can track the rates of response to ads, referrals, direct mail, networking efforts etc. By tracking the rates of response to each promotional effort you'll be able to determine where your marketing is paying off (or not). If you can't measure your marketing, you have to questions if it's worth doing."

9. Pulling from Direct Mail – End a page with an incomplete sentence to make readers want to turn the page. Use subheads. If the subheads are interesting enough they will draw the reader into the letter. Use short testimonials. Readers love to see what other people have to say about you.

10. Unlikely Envelopes – Remember that the post office will send almost anything you stick a stamp to. Anything from coconuts to canisters – so go ahead, get creative with your packaging.

11. Internet Inconsistency – To keep both prospects and surfers coming back to your web site time after time, put useful information there and keep it updated. Content is king on the Internet. In traditional advertising it's usually wise to have 90% of the piece for persuasion and 10% for information, marketing on the Net is just reverse: 90% information and 10% persuasion.

12. Newsgroup Netiquette – You can solicit clients through newsgroups on the Internet by surfing the bulletin boards relevant to your target market and answering the questions of users. Be careful to note the newsgroup's rules on advertising and spamming however, you don't want to be the recipient of "flame" e-mails.

13. Signature Selling – Using an e-mail signature (a small blurb that automatically attaches to the end of your e-mail and newsgroup postings) allows you to add information about you, your company, or your services. This addendum helps spread the word about your offerings without actually selling.

14. The Name Game – The best names are locked directly to a service benefit or selling proposition. Describe your service or connect the name with your strategy (like speed, customization etc.).

15. About Your Backside – Watch what happens when you hand out your business card. Frequently the

recipient looks at both the front and back. Use the back to add a message, an appropriate quote, or pertinent information.

16. "The key word is flexibility, the ability to adapt constantly. Darwin said it clearly. People thought that he mainly talked about survival of the fittest. What he said was that the species that survive are usually not the smartest or the strongest, but the ones most responsive to change. So being attentive to customers and potential partners is my best advice – after, of course, perseverance and patience." Philippe Kahn, founder of Borland International and Starfish Software.

17. Disk Delivery – Why not show your potential clients your services with a CD business card. These petit disks are the size of a business card and allow you to be seen and heard in full digital glory. The disks are inexpensive to copy (about a dollar) and can usually be produced for under $2,000. Compare this to graphic design costs, printing costs, postage costs, and time and effort.

18. Unique Business Cards – Instead of printing your business cards on standard stock, explore alternative materials and styles. Use translucent paper, shiny paper, textured paper, etc. Use both sides, have the cards cut into a unique shape that is appropriate for your specialty. Even pop-up cards or 3-D images

would work to show the progression of dispute to content.

19. Just the Fax – Every day your company sends faxes, usually on cover sheet with empty space just begging to be used. So why not make faxes work twice as hard for you? Redesign your fax cover sheets to include news about your company for customers and contacts.

20. Network Your Chamber – Your local Chamber of Commerce is a great way to meet people who can provide you with referrals and business. Your dues also provide you with the benefit of the Chamber's membership list (a great way to add on to your database).

21. "The moment you make a mistake in pricing, you're eating into your reputation or your profits."
Katharine Paine, founder of the Delahaye Group, Hampton Falls, N.H.

22. Under-pricing Upsets – If you price your services too low, you run the risk of losing potential clients who believe that a consumer always gets what they pay for. Consumers assume that low cost equals low quality.

23. "The secret is to know your customer. Segment your target as tightly as possible. Determine exactly who your customers are, both demographically and

psycho graphically. Match your customer with your medium. Choose only those media that reach your potential customers, and no others. Reaching anyone else is waste." Robert Grede, author of Naked Marketing, the Bare Essentials.

24. Establishing Authority – Turn your expertise into authority and referrals. If your specialty is hearing construction cases, offer a free (or nominal) seminar that touts the benefits of ADR for the construction industry. Be sure you get the attendees contact information for your database.

25. Work and Socialize at the Same Time – Networking at both business and social events is an extremely powerful method of creating word-of-mouth advertising, referrals, and clients. Be sure to arrive with plenty of business cards and a pen. Try to spend more than 10 minutes with each person you meet and remember to listen more than you talk. Take discreet notes on the back of their business card so that you can more easily and effectively follow up with them (in a timely manner please.)

26. Tag! You're It – When you get someone's answering machine and decide to leave a message there are several ways to ensure a return call. Don't give your sales pitch to the machine. Your objective should be to pitch in person. You can leave your just your first name and phone number (in a very business-like

manner). Calls are returned in inverse proportion to the amount of information left by the caller.

27. Your Unique Selling Proposition is Your Personal Philosophy – Tell them like it is!
    a. What specifics do you have to offer?
    b. What do you do that makes you special?
    c. What will you do for them that will make them want to do business with you?

28. Tag Lines – A good company "tag line" is a short phrase telling clients who you are and what you do. It will help you to both win the mindshare of your customers and portray your corporate image.

29. Mission Statements are Good Marketing Tools – They help cement the relationship between you and you clients and present a way to establish and understand your company goals.

30. Put your Mission Statement on your business cards, company stationary, your advertising, packaging, and newsletters.

31. Corporate Logo – A company logo is the fingerprint for your business. A good logo will establish brand name recognition add to the image you're trying to build, as well as reinforce you're marketing efforts.

32. Why are business cards important? Think of business cards as a mobile, one-dimensional version of

yourself. A miniature you not waiting to happen but present and accounted for as long as the card is in circulation.

33. How do you make your business card stand out from the others?
    a. Color stock
    b. Mylar stock
    c. Create a fold cover
    d. Make it in the shape of your product or service
    e. Be unique.

34. Business Card "Do's"
    a. Include all contact information
    b. Use your company "tag line"
    c. Include your logo
    d. Use the back for a your mission statement
    e. Gold and silver portray elegance.
    f. Think of your business card as a virtual "you."

35. Business Card "Don'ts"
    a. If your contact information changes, do not cross them out and write in the new ones by hand.
    b. Don't use neon card stock
    c. Don't use all capital letters, they are hard to read.
    d. Don't use too many typefaces.

36. Sign all business letters personally. Use blue ink.

37. Written Brochures – Another part of your arsenal. The more your name is seen and heard, the more people will come to know you.

38. Written Brochures – Position your company, Initiate dialogue, Amplify your sales letters, Lend credibility when professionally executed, Act as a direct-mail piece when prospecting anytime anyplace.

39. Key Elements of a Successful Written Brochure – Create a brochure with your prospect in mind, not your ego. Include a call to action, ask for an order, a meeting time, or offer a way to request more information. Include testimonials to show clients past performance.

40. Make It Personal – Include a personalized "Post It" note or letter when sending out any type of marketing material.

41. What are the biggest mistakes people make when designing their brochures?: The single biggest mistake you can make when designing a brochure is to highlight features, instead of showing benefits. Do not toot your own horn. Instead, show your client you can solve their problems and fill their needs.

42. Newsletters are a powerful way of developing name

brand recognition and telling people who you are and what products and services you have to offer.

43. Are you a professional? Well then write an article. Writing an article on your field of expertise automatically puts you on the top of an experts list and is a good way to reach thousands of people for free with one effort. In addition it also affords great name recognition.

44. When Marketing – Personalize it. Make it brief. Make it consistent. Keep efforts positive orientated and focus on the benefits.

45. What kind of publications will take your articles? Trade Journals and Consumer publications are the best avenue for you to work with. They will be the most likely to take your article, while simultaneously enabling you to reach your target market.

46. Always remember that people interested in success are always open to tips, trends, hints, and help.

47. Write a regular column – A simultaneous symphony of words and ideas. It will no doubt be difficult to get your column published by the New York Times. But is that really the best place to publish your column anyway? Try other avenues of papers like Dailies, Weeklies, Monthlies, Quarterlies, and free local papers where your work won't be buried on the back

of page 21A. Remember it's better to focus your efforts and remain steadfast on reaching your specific target market than marketing to the general populous at large.

48. Syndicate Your Way – Try to get your column picked up by a syndicate. Use their leverage to help you reach a larger audience.

49. Test the Waters First – Only Print 50,000 brochures after proven success. Before you rush out and print 50,000 copies of your newly designed brochure, it would be a wise idea to run a test print and send out 5,000 mailings first to gauge the response you'll get. Determine a range of acceptable responses to your mailings. This will help save valuable time, money and resources.

50. Set Up a Fax On Demand (FOD) System – Fax on demand is an easy to use, cost effective way to help your company be more responsive, professional, and profitable. There are several broadcast fax and fax on demand services available. Outsourcing this service will benefit you and your clients by letting the pros do what they do best.

51. Hold Buttons – Use your silent downtime to your advantage. 94% of all add budgets are spent to induce calls, only 6% is spent to handle calls already made. 88% of all business callers will hang up if

forced to hold. 34% of hang up's won't call again. With a strategic hold marketing campaign 85% of callers will keep holding to hear the messages you specifically designate for them to listen to.

52. Pictures Are In Fact Worth a 1000 Words – Consider this simple concept the next time your creating advertisements or brochures.

53. Six Powerful Things to Keep in Mind When Writing Sales Letters – Take the best, most powerful thing you have to say and launch it at the beginning. Your headline is the most important part of the ad. The headline is the first thing people will see and read. Speak directly to your readers. Know who your prospect is. Prove the points you make and be specific.

54. Use your mailing envelope to tease and promote the contents inside. Simply mailing out a brochure or sales letter is not enough if you can't even get your prospect to open the package. You must invoke their desire to peruse the contents inside. Write a note from the president of the company telling them what's inside. Include previous client testimonials, restate the bonus offer, and express their actions as needing to be urgent.

55. Postcard Campaigns – Maximize the exposure of your name, service, or product to your target audi-

ence. Postcards are less expensive than brochure mailings and don't need to be opened like an envelope. Use three questions to get your reader thinking about your benefits and don't forget to include your company tag line and logo for brand name recognition.

56. Create a Strategic Marketing Plan – Sure there's a lot involved to make sure that your marketing efforts work. What's the best way to make sure that you cover all the major do's and don'ts? First start by creating a plan of attack. Define your goals and devise the actions necessary to reach them. Maintain check lists to help you remember all of the important points.

57. "I am the world's worst salesman. Therefore, I must make it easy for people to buy." F.W. Woolworth

FIVE • WAYS TO SAVE MONEY IN MARKETING!

In general, your mother was right. You get what you pay for, especially in marketing. It is very difficult to do good marketing without spending any money. Here are a few ideas for you to try.

▶ Plan to Plan. Write a Marketing Plan, or get someone to help you write one, so that you can make a commitment to spend nothing on marketing without knowing why and considering an alternative. The more time you spend on developing a strategy and designing your program based on it, the more cost-effective and economical your marketing will be.

▸ Target Your Audience. Don't waste time and money marketing to people or organizations that will never become customers. Identify your target marketing and attack it.

▸ Be Creative. All things being equal, the more you market the more you sell. Outsmart your competition on the creative playing field, and you'll walk away the winner.

▸ Use New Mediums. If you structured your campaign to use direct mail alone, try the Worldwide Web to mix things up. Our industry rarely uses national and regional magazines – give them a try. (Start small to make sure the time and money investment will pay off). Call us for a list of periodicals and some general periodical advertising advice.

▸ Don't Give Away Your Services. To be competitive in the marketplace you must have competitive pricing. By giving away your services, you do not create a competitive or professional image of you and your practice. Look professional, act professional, and charge professional prices. You'll be amazed at the outcome!! (see volunteerism below)

▶ Volunteerism. A standard in our industry.
Volunteerism is a fantastic marketing tool, learning
tool, and social responsibility. You should never quit
giving your community the benefit of your training
and experience … but you can make it profitable.
Volunteer for organizations that would and could
become clients or referrals. Don't volunteer for an
equestrian association if your ADR specialty is
human resources and labor law. Volunteer within
your target market and/or for people who could and
would provide referrals for your practice.

Glossary of
Words That Sell

▼ ▼ ▼

PHRASES

1. The _____ advantage
2. Only _____ gives you
3. For the finest in _____ , look to _____
4. Expect only the best…
5. The _____ experts.
6. For those who insist on the best
7. Finally there's a better way to…
8. _____ is our business
9. Now more than ever you need _____
10. _____ reasons why you need…
11. Will you be ready for the…
12. Will you be ready for the next time…
13. What's the best investment you could make?
14. How much is your company spending on...?
15. What's the most effective way to...
16. It's no secret that…

17. If you're like most people, you probably…
18. Within 30 days from today, you could change the way you…
19. Believe it or not…
20. We live in an increasingly complex society…
21. Today more than ever…
22. It's a fact of life that…
23. Its' never too late to…
24. It isn't enough to be…
25. _____ may determine the future of your business…
26. We've got the solution for you…
27. Capture the…
28. Discover the…
29. Learn about the…
30. This we promise
31. One thing is for sure…
32. What does this mean for you?

STATUS

1. The Rolls Royce of…
2. Class
3. Highest ranking
4. Elite
5. Exclusive

DESCRIPTIVE WORDS

1. Comprehensive
2. The ultimate

3. The only _____ you'll ever need…
4. Leaves no stone unturned
5. Simplifies
6. Facilitates
7. Clarifies
8. Easily adaptable
9. Reputable
10. Flexible
11. Respected
12. Prestigious
13. Premier
14. A positive force in bringing about…
15. Outstanding
16. Honored
17. Accomplished
18. Talented
19. Veteran
20. For over _____ years
21. Since (date)
22. Mastery of…
23. Integrity
24. Genuine

MORE

1. Your passport to…
2. Preferred by more…
3. Strong
4. No nonsense
5. Tough

6. Gets results

7. Never lets up

8. Raises the bar…

9. Raises

10. Produces…

11. Provides

12. Provides a higher level of service…

13. Creates…

14. Our job is to help you…

15. Lets you…

16. Aids…

17. Solves…

18. Advises…

19. Performs...

SUPERIOR

1. The highest quality

2. The finest…

3. The greatest…

4. The foremost…

5. Unsurpassed

6. First class

7. Excellent

8. Superb

9. Outstanding

10. Unparalleled

11. Paramount

12. The better way to…

13. Excels

14. Supreme

15. The standards by which others are judged...

PURE PERSUASION

1. We think you'll find that...

2. We think you'll agree...

3. We stand behind our claims...

4. Ready to prove everything we claim...

THE MOMENT OF DECISION

1. This is your moment!!

2. Now is the time.

3. Make a winning decision

4. Take this important first step

5. Decide for yourself

6. Make this a turning point for your company...

IMAGE

1. Our dedication to...

2. We serve

3. We uphold

4. We're dedicated to...

5. We meet every challenge

Glossary of Internet Terms

▼ ▼ ▼

Address Book: A personal directory of e-mail addresses stored and maintained with one's e-mail program.

Alias: A collection of e-mail addresses stored under one name to facilitate addressing mail to a particular group of users.

Archie: A search utility that surveys all Ftp sites once a month and builds an index of all software at those sites. The index is stored on an Archie server on the Net. Short for "archiver".

Browser: A program used to access and view information on World-wide Web, Gopher, or WAIS servers.

Bulletin board system (BBS): Any computer system and software with one or more telephone lines that will accept a phone call from another computer at any time with little or no prior arrangement for access.

Chat room: An area in an online service or BBS where several users can meet simultaneously and exchange typed messages.

Conference: A large chat session that features a main speaker and an audience that asks questions.

Cybernaut: One who uses the Internet.

Cyberspace: Another name for the online universe.

Directory: A named subsection of the storage space on a server or computer storage disk.

Discussion group: An electronic message board on an online service, BBS, or the Net that contains messages focusing on a specific topic.

Domain: A category of network on the Internet, or a specific network name, called a domain name. Every Internet address has a suffix that indicates its domain. Some common domain suffixes are .com (commercial organizations), .edu (education), .gov (government), and .net (network).

Domain name service: A service offered by as ISP that registers customers' servers as distinct Internet domains.

Download: To retrieve a file from an online service, BBS, Internet server.

Electronic mail (e-mail): A means of exchanging typed messages between computer users in which messages are sent to specific addresses and stored in mail boxes.

E-zine: See "'Zine".

FAQs (Frequently Asked Questions): A collection of frequent questions about a particular discussion group, bulletin board, Internet service, or other subject.

Flame: To send a poison-pen email letter to another Internet user, usually someone who has violated netiquette.

Forum: The name used for a discussion group on an online service or BBS.

From box: The space at the top of an e-mail message that indicates who the message is from.

Ftp (File transfer protocol): A program that allows you to transfer files to and from other computers on the Internet.

Gopher: A method of locating information in the Internet. Also a type of server that uses that location method and a software program used to locate such servers.

Header: The portion of an e-mail document that contains the mailing address (or To address), the return address (or from address), and subject information.

Hit: A specific access of a server by a user. Server traffic is some times measured in hits per hour or hits per day. An active Net server has thousands of hits per day. That is, it is accessed thousands of times per day by various users.

Home page: The introductory or menu page of a web site. A home page usually contains the site's name and a directory of its contents.

Host: The space that you "rent" or park your web site.

HTML (Hypertext markup language): The programming language used to store and present information on the Worldwide Web servers.

HTTP (Hypertext Transfer Protocol): The communications protocol, or set of technical rules, through which Worldwide Web information is linked on the Internet.

Hypertext link: An automatic link on the Worldwide Web that connects a word, phrase or picture on one server with another server. When a user selects a linked phrase or picture that user is automatically connected to the server to which it is linked.

Image map: A graphic image on the Worldwide Web that contains several hypertext links, each of which is located in a different part of the image.

Internet: An international data communications pathway that links thousands of computer networks together. Also known as the Net.

Internet service provider (ISP): A company or organization that offers Internet access to customers for a fee. Also called an IAP, or Internet access provider.

Lurker: Someone who monitors a mailing list, forum, or newsgroup without posting to it.

Mailbot: A program that responds automatically to incoming e-mail. A mailbot receives e-mail messages and then replies to them automatically by sending messages or files to their authors.

Mailing list: An electronic discussion carried out with e-mail messages rather than with an electronic message board. Rather than posting a message to a discussion board, you send it to the mailing list's email address. All subscribers to a mailing list receive copies of all messages sent to that list's address.

Mailing list manager: A program that collects and distributes e-mail messages to a mailing list.

Modem: A device that allows a computer to connect with other computes over standard telephone lines by dialing phone numbers.

Navigator: A browser used to search for and display information on the Internet.

Net: Shorthand for Internet

Netiquette: Rules of conduct for Internet users.

Netizen: Someone who uses the Internet; a member of the Internet community of users.

Netscape: Λ Worldwide Web browser program, and the name of the company that makes it.

Newbie: A newcomer to the Internet or to an online service.

Newsgroup: A message board on the Internet that focuses on a particular subject. Also known as a Usenet newsgroup.

Newsreader: A program that allows you to read newsgroups on the Internet.

Online service: A large commercial bulletin board system that accommodates hundreds or thousands of users at once, offers a wide variety of services and information, and charges a monthly subscription fee.

Post: To send a message to a discussion group or mailing list. A message posted to a discussion group or sent to a mailing list.

Server: A computer that stores files and makes them available to other users on a network or on the Internet.

Server log: A record of users accessing a particular server.

Signature: A block of information used to sign the end of an e-mail or discussion group message. It usually includes an author name, company name, e-mail address, and other information.

Site: A distinct location for information on the Internet.

Snail mail: A cybernaut's term for paper or postal mail.

Spam: To cross-post or mass-mail unsolicited electronic messages to a large number of discussion groups or individuals on the Net.

Special interest groups (SIG): Another name for a forum or discussion group most frequently used on CompuServe.

Storefront: A fixed location on the Worldwide Web, an online service, or a bulletin board system that stores a collection of information about your business which can be accessed by others at any time.

T1, T2, T3, and T4 lines: High-speed telephone lines that are leased from a telephone company and provide an ongoing connection for data transfers.

Telnet: A program that allows you to log on to other computers or bulletin board systems on the Internet and run programs on them remotely.

Top menu: The menu on a server that functions as its table of contents.

Unix: A powerful computer operating system that is used on many Internet servers.

Upload: To transfer a file from your PC to a BBS, online service, or a server on the Net.

URL (Universal Resource Locator): A standardized address format used for Internet addresses, especially for Worldwide Web addresses.

Usenet: The largest collection of newsgroups on the Internet.

WAIS (Wide Area Information Servers): A system for searching for files or programs via groups of keywords. Also, servers that are set up to be accessed by that system.

Web: Shorthand for Worldwide Web.

Web site: A storefront located on the Web.

Worldwide Web: A collection of information located on many Internet servers, which can be accessed with a browser or by navigating via hypertext links.

'*Zine*: An electronic publication on one very specific topic published by one person or a handful of people and distributed at intervals for free over the Internet:

Glossary of Marketing Terms
▼ ▼ ▼

Advertising: Paid commercial messages (in any medium) designed to inform, persuade, or remind potential or actual customers about a product or service.

After-sale actions: Those actions you take to retain a customer by providing additional benefits after the sale has been completed.

AIDA: An acronym for a sales "rule." Gain the prospect's "Attention," arouse their "Interest," pique their "Desire," and move them to take "Action."

Banners: Internet advertising you run on carefully selected sites where you expect to find your prospects and customers. The ads usually look like a banner (hence the name) and call attention to your own Web site.

Behavioral segmentation: A market segmentation technique based on different behaviors exhibited by consumers.

Benefits: What people buy, the "what's in it for me" that all consumers seek, as distinguished from features, the characteristics of a product or service that deliver benefits.

Branding: The techniques used to establish a brand name for a commodity. Successful branding examples: Coco-Cola, Kleenex, Xerox, Perdue Chicken. Currently used mainly in e-commerce for companies such as eBay, Amazon, and iVillage.

Browser: Software such as Netscape or Microsoft's Internet Explorer that is used to examine various Internet resources.

Clipping service: A service business that clips items and references from periodicals and other sources (increasingly from the Internet) according to parameters set by the client.

Collateral material: Promotional material in addition to paid advertising, which includes brochures, flyers, business cards, stationery, and other image pieces.

Competitive edge: Your competitive advantages over your most direct competitors.

Consumer demand: The aggregate demand for a given product or service in a defined market area. This is an important measure to determine for your product or service.

Core competency: What your business does best; its most important and central activity.

Cost structure: The analysis of all the cost factors in the production or marketing of a product or service, including burden or share of overhead.

Customer need: Primary needs (physiological, safety, and security) and secondary needs (such as self-expression or status) have a big impact on buyer behavior. You should ascertain what customer needs your particular service satisfies.

Database marketing: Compiling detailed consumer information in a database format allows marketers to precisely allocate marketing efforts to the most productive market segments for a given product or family of products.

Deliverable: The tangibles that you actually give to the customer, such as a consultant's bound report.

Demographics: The study of the characteristics of a population, such as age, gender, religious affiliation, income.

Direct mail: A marketing technique in which sales are generated by sending a "direct mail" package (advertisement, product offer, response device) to a mailing list.

Direct response marketing: A variant of direct marketing in which the prospect qualifies him or herself by responding to an offer. The offer may be presented as a coupon, a direct mail package, an 800 number in a space advertisement or other means. By responding, the prospect indicates an interest in the offer.

E-commerce: Short for "electronic commerce," and includes I-commerce as well as other forms of electronic commerce.

Elasticity: If a market is sensitive to price changes, buying less if the price rises or more if it falls, that market is said to be elastic. An inelastic market is relatively unaffected by small price changes.

Ethnic marketing: Marketing promotions aimed at a specific ethnic group, such as Hispanics or Asians.

Facility brochure: A brochure that explains the full range of services or products a firm provides its customers.

Focus group: A market research technique in which a small number of people are brought together and interviewed, under controlled conditions, about their perceptions of the value of a product or service.

Geographic segmentation: Market segmentation based on a geographic area. A sole proprietor mediation practice might have a geographic area of a few blocks, whereas AAA or JAMS covers the majority of the United States.

Home page: The main Web page, or Web site, for an individual, organization, or business.

I-commerce: Internet-based commerce, a narrower term than e-commerce, though less commonly used.

Image: The managed perception of the general public of a person, business, or institution. This is an essential piece of the marketing mix.

Internet: The collection of interconnected computer based networks that all use a common protocol (TCP/IP) to share data.

Links: On the Internet, a method of connecting ("linking") one Web page with other Web pages, whether in the same or other networks.

Market gaps: Areas in your market where there are untapped opportunities for you to take advantage of.

Market niche: A smaller fragment of a larger market that's especially suited to your unique abilities and your business's product or service.

Market segmentation: A method of organizing and categorizing people or organizations that buy your products or services.

Market share: A portion, usually expressed as a percentage, of a market that a business operates in.

Marketing strategy: Action steps that deliberate how your company will reach its marketing goals.

Marketing: All the activities involved in moving products and services from the producer to the consumer, including advertising, sales, packaging, and pricing.

Meta tags: Words that appear in the header of a Web site's home page.

Multi-level marketing: A method of distributing good and services that incorporates network marketing direct selling, and person-to-person marketing.

Networking: A promotional tool for expanding your group of contacts, as well as building relationships in your field and in others.

Positioning: How you differentiate your services from those of your competitors and determine what market niche to fill.

Price ceiling and price floor: The "right" price for your goods and services will float somewhere between a "price ceiling" (what the traffic will bear) and a "price floor" (high enough to cover your cost and profit needs).

Profit: The return on a business undertaking received after all operating expenses are paid.

Promotion: How you make your market aware of your product or service. Promotion includes advertising, public relations, special events, newsletter, networking, and public speaking.

Prospecting: A process of selecting likely customers from a group.

Psychographics: A method of segmenting a market that looks at a group's behavior patterns, attitudes, and expectations.

Public relations: Methods and activities that promote a favorable relationship with the public.

Qualify: Establishing certain characteristics that prospective customers must meet.

Socio-cultural segmentation: A method of segmenting a market that takes into account a group's religions, national origin, race, social class, and marital status.

SWOT analysis: A method of analyzing a business that looks at its "Strengths, Weaknesses, Opportunites, and Threats." This helps a business decide what to emphasize and what not to emphasize, and takes into account both internal and external forces.

Target market: Those people or organizations in your market who are most likely to buy from you.

Telemarketing: A sales tool that's also called telephone marketing.

Trends: The inclination of a market to favor a particular product or product feature.

URL: An acronym for Uniform Resource Locator, which is an Internet address.

Web site: See Home page

Business Plan

BUSINESS PLAN TEMPLATE

The following pages provide a template for writing and formatting your own business plan.

TITLE PAGE

It's a great idea to put a color picture of your product right on the front. But leave room for the following information:

[Your Company Name]

Month, 20xx
[month and year issued]

Business Plan Copy Number [x]
This document is confidential. It is not for re-distribution.

[Name of point man in financing]
[Title]
[Address]
[City, State ZIP]
[Phone]
[e-mail]
[company home page URL]

This is a business plan. It does not imply an offering of Securities.

TABLE OF CONTENTS

Be sure to modify the page numbers when you've finished your Business Plan.

EXECUTIVE SUMMARY

If the executive summary doesn't succeed, your business plan will never sell investors. We recommend that you write the summary first and use it as a template for the plan as a whole. Since one of its primary functions is to capture the investor's attention, the summary should be no longer than two pages. The shorter the better.

Mission

Our company's mission is to [describe your ultimate goal, or insert your mission statement].

Company

[The Company] was founded in [date] and [describe what your business does, such as baby products manufacturer, distributor of pencils, provider of medical services]. It is a [legal form of your company, such as LLC, S-Corporation, C-Corporation, Partnership, Proprietorship]. Our principal offices are located at [x].

Business

We make [describe product, or service that you make or provide].

Our company is at the [seed, start-up, growth] stage of business, having just [developed our first product, hired our first salesman, booked our first national order].

In the most recent [period], our company achieved sales of [x], and showed a [profit, loss, break-even]. With the financing contemplated herein, our company expected to achieve [x] in sales and [x] in pretax profits in 19[xx] and achieve [x] in sales and [x] in pretax profits in

19[xx+1]. We can achieve this because the funds will allow us to [describe what you will do with the funds, such as a) marketing for your new product, b) build or expand facilities to meet increased demand, c) add retail locations or others means of distribution, d) increase research and development for new products or to improve existing ones.

Product or Service

Tell us about your product or service in terms we can understand.

[The company] produces the following products; [list products here briefly, in order of highest sales or significance in product line].

Alternatively, [The company] delivers the following services; [list services here briefly, in order of highest sales or significance in product line].

Presently, our [product or service] is in the [introductory, growth, maturity] stage. We plan to follow this [product or service] with extensions to our line which include [x,y,and z].

Critical factors in the [production of our product, or delivery of our service are [x, and y]. Our [product or service] is unique because [x,y,or z] and/or we have an advantage in the marketplace because of our [patent, speed to market, brand name].

The Market

We define our market as [manufacture and sale of writing and drawing instruments, low fat cheese, oral care products]. This market was approximately [$x] at [wholesale or retail] last [period available], according to [site resource], and is expected to grow to [$x] by the year [x], according to [site resource].

Who are your customers? Where are they, and how do you reach them? Are they buying your product / service from someone else? How will you educate customers to buy from you? Why will they care?

Competition

We compete directly with [name competition]. or We have no direct competition, but there are alternatives to our [product or service] in the marketplace. Our [product or service] is unique because of [x] and/or we have a competitive advantage because of our [speed to market, established brand name, low cost producer status].

Risk/Opportunity

The greatest risks we have in our business today are [market risk, pricing risk, product risk, management risk]. We feel we can over-come these risks because of [x].

The opportunities before us are significant; we have the opportunity to [dominate a niche in the marketplace, become a major force in the industry] if we can [x].

Management Team

Our team has the following members to achieve our plan. [x] men and women who have a combined [x] years of experience; [y] years in marketing, [y] years in product development, and [y] years in [other disciplines].

Capital Requirements

We seek [$] of additional [equity, sub-debt, or senior financing] which will enable us to [describe why you need the funds, and why the opportunity is exciting]. We can provide and exit for this [loan, investment] within [x] years by [a dividend of excess profits, recapitalizations, sale of company, or public offering].

Financial Plan

At this point the investor must have a clear idea of where your business stands today. If you bore him or make the information he needs hard to find, you get canned. You must provide a snapshot, however sparse, of your financial position.

Sales Summary

At this point the investor must have a clear idea of where your business stands today. If you bore him or make the information he needs hard to find, you get canned. You must provide a snapshot, however sparse, of your financial position.

	Last Year	This Year	Next Year	Year Two
Sales:				
Gross profit:				
Pre-tax:				

Balance Sheet Summary

Assets:
Liabilities:
Book Value:

In [x] years we will provide an exit, which we expect to be in the form of [sale to a competitor, initial public offering, distribution of profits] or perhaps [z]. We expect to be able to acheive this in [b months / years].

MISSION

Mission Statement

Our goal is to become [describe your ultimate goal, or insert your mission statement; example; the leading manufacturer and marketer of branded in-line skate replacement wheels or the first name in low fat cheese].

We aspire to carry a reputation in the marketplace for developing and delivering [time saving, better-way products sold at a fair price for uses in the {x} market]. We can achieve this by [cutting edge product development, close understanding of market trends and needs, innovative and profitable merchandising and packaging].

To accomplish our goal, [your company name] needs [capital, management talent, larger, more efficient facilities].

In pursuit of our goal, we resolve to treat stakeholders, customers, and the community with [description of the reputation your company seeks]. These groups see our company as providing [describe benefits to each group of being associated with your company].

THE COMPANY

[The Company] was founded in [date] and [describe what your business does, such as baby products manufacturer, distributor of pencils, provider of medical services]. The legal name of the business is [x]. Include dba in the legal name.

It is a [legal form of your company, such as LLC, S-Corporation, C-Corporation, Partnership, Proprietorship]. Our principal offices are located at [list primary address as well as any other facilities]. We have approximately [x] square feet of office space and [x] square feet of [factory or warehouse]. Our current capacity is [x] units per month. If we exceed [x] units per month, we will need additional space. We expect this facility to be adequate for the company's needs for [two years, a year, a week] after funding.

Regulations and permits- cut if inappropriate.

[Your Company Name] operates in the [toxic waste, weapons and armaments, genetic engineering, explosives] industry, or [uses controlled substances in the manufacturing process or delivery of service], and falls under the jurisdiction of the [name government agency].

[Your Company Name] has all necessary permits to operate, and has an up-to-date record of inspections. These permits include; [list briefly here]. These agencies regulate our business in the following manner; [we must document and account for uses and disposal of all toxic materials or we must document and background check all employees with access to the launch codes for our missiles].

Strategic   Alliances

The leverage from relationships can be appealing to investors. Explain how you work with others to improve your performance.

[Your Company Name] has developed important and profitable strategic alliances with the following larger, more established business; [describe each company, it's position in the marketplace, the details of the alliance, and what risks are involved in the alliance]. For example, we have developed marketing agreements with [x], the [market leader in gummed erasers] which will enable us to sell, along side them, our [extra messy children's pencils].

The side by side positioning at retail, as well as the ability to share wholesale sales leads with their established customer base can help us penetrate the market more quickly.

The risk in the relationship is that they may [decide to sell pencils themselves] and cut us out of the process.

Another type of strategic relationship that benefits the company is our development joint venture with [x]. We would never be able to fund the research of the new [low fat Swiss cheese that melts smoothly], but with access to their prior research in [smooth melting cheddar] we cut our development time in half. By using some of their [equipment, or people] who we not being utilized fully, we were able to avoid the expense of [major capital expenditures, additions to the payroll]. We have agreed to pay a royalty of [x] to this development partner for their role in this products ultimate success.

We have a strategic relationship with a number of suppliers. In exchange for a blanket commitment to purchase [more than 80% of our supply of a specific raw material from them], they have agreed to [not make it available to the market at large for six months, or to give us a preferential price].

[Your Company Name] also has strategic Original Equipment Manufacturer relationships with a number of customers. This allows us to sell a large and steady volume of [in-line skate wheels] to [boot manufacturers, who use them to sell complete skate sets]. This gets many units of our product out in to the marketplace, however, it provides little or no brand awareness for us.

THE BUSINESS

[Your Company Name] is a [manufacturer, distributor, marketer, service provider] of [describe your product or service].

Our company is at the [seed, start-up, growth] stage of business, having just [developed our first product, hired our first salesman, booked our first national order].

Product or Service

Explain how your product works or how the service is used. What burning marketplace needs are addressed by your product? What value do you add to the product?

[The company] produces the following products; [list products here, in order of highest sales or significance in product line]. Be sure to refer readers to product pictures, diagrams, patents, and other descriptive material.

Or, Alternatively

[The company] delivers the following services; [list services here briefly, in order of highest sales or significance in product line]. Be sure to refer readers to brochures and material describing your service.

Presently, our [product or service] is in the [introductory, growth, maturity] stage. We first developed our [product or service] in 19[xx] and have made [x] improvements and redesigns since then. Provide a history of product developments, introductions, and improvements leading up to the present day. Table form may be appropriate.

Unique features or proprietary aspects of product

This is a crucial paragraph. Investors must see something unique, proprietary, or protected about your product or service.

Our products are unique because of [of secret ingredient, our patented process, our proprietary manufacturing process].

Others in the market are able to provide somewhat similar [products or services], but we are able to differentiate ourselves in the market because of [x].

We have [applied, been granted, licensed] a patent for [x], an abstract of which can be found in appendix [x]. We have integrated this into our process which others will not be able to duplicate. Our lead product, [x] addresses the following customer needs [x] and delivers [x] benefits to customers.

Tell us about the unique value-added characteristics your product line or process provides to customers and how these characteristics translate into a competitive advantage for your company.

Research and Development

Our research and development is headed by [name of person or contractor] whose major objective is to use market input to [develop products that solve problems or provide superior benefits to customers]. Last [period], our R&D yielded the following products and innovations; [list products or innovations]. [Your Company name] has spent [% of revenues, or absolute $] in the past year in R&D, and plans to spend [% or $] in the next [period].

Our R&D occasionally yields innovation without input from customers or the marketplace. Our product selection criteria in this case is as follows; [relatively low investment requirements, positive return on investment, fit with present strategy, feasibilty of development and production, relatively low risk, time to see intended results, buyer in common]. Our R&D will require additional resources in the future. These will include [people, capital expenditures] to [speed up development process, test results more efficiently].

New and Follow-on Products

Responding to market needs, we plan to follow [product or service] with extensions to our line which include [x,y,and z].

Our target introduction dates for these products are [x,y,and z], which corresponds with [a major trade show, industry event]. In addition, we plan to introduce the following new products in the upcoming season; [x,y,and z].

Production

Our [product, service] is [manufactured in house, assembled in house from components from various vendors, (service) provided by our staff, or subcontracted to field consultants]. [Raw materials, sub-assemblies, components] used in our products are readily available from a variety of manufacturers who can meet our quality standards.

Critical factors in the [production of our product, or delivery of our service are [x, and y].

Enumerate and explain capital equipment, material, and labor requirements. Are the above items readily available? Do you have multiple supply sources? List inventory requirements, quality and technical specifications, hazardous materials.

Uniqueness

Our [product or service] is unique because [x,y,or z] and/or we have an advantage in the marketplace because of our [patent, speed to market, brand name].

THE MARKET

Sad fact: this is the most crucial but worst-prepared section of most business plans.

Market   Definition

What markets are you competing in? If you make glove-compartment hinges, don't gush about the $80 billion automobile market. You make hinges — not cars — for that market, so tell us how many hinges were sold last year. Are there other markets where you sell your products?

We [expect to compete, are competing] in the [define niche] of the [define industry]. This market was approximately [$x] at [wholesale or retail] last [period available], according to [site resource]. We believe, the major future trend in the industry will be toward [environmentally oriented, miniaturized, high quality, value oriented] product offerings.

Market research [cite source] suggests this market will [grow/shrink] to [$x] by the year [19xx]. We expect the niche in which we compete to [grow, shrink, remain stagnant] during this time. The major forces affecting this change will be [falling cost of computers, explosion of home based businesses, tendency for baby boomers to have less kids- and pamper their pets]. The area of greatest growth within the industry will be [x].

Identify where you got this information, and how up to date it is.

Market   Segment

We define our market segment as [the writing and drawing instrument segment of the school/home/office products industry, the low fat dairy products segment of the food industry]. This segment has been [volatile, steady] in the last few years. Industry experts [name them] forecast [x] for the industry in the next few years.

The major market segments [segment a, segment b, segment c]. List, in general, the types of customers you are likely to reach (retailers, electrical contractors, catalog buyers, etc.)] The [a] segment of the market is based on [product type] that retail in the [x to y] price range. Most of the sales in the segment are delivered through the [catalogs, retailers, manufacturers reps, OEM's].

A typical customer for our product is a person who current may use [alternative product or service] for [what purpose]. They are motivated to buy our product because of [its value, its quality, its usefulness]. We know this from [customer responses, trade show input, ad inquiries] and feel our customers perceive our products as [good value, superior performance, great taste].

Our product, does, however, have the following weaknesses; [higher price point than most other cheeses, weak brand identity in a commodity market]. We are working to position our product as [x] in order to reduce this vulnerability.

Marketing

Our marketing plan is based on the following fundamentals;
We expect to penetrate the [x] segment of the market[s] and achieve this by using the [retail, mail order, multi-level marketing, internet] as

our primary distribution channel[s]. In time, we plan to capture [%] share of the market.

Position

We will position our product as [good value for price, top quality, cheap and fun], which is a position not presently being addressed by the competition. One demographic group in particular, the [elderly, hispanic, generationX, techies] has a particular need for this product, and we tailor our positioning accordingly.

Pricing

Our pricing strategy is [describe policy or, at least philosophy]. *Is this pricing based on cost? Gross margin objectives? Market?*

We arrive at our pricing based on [cost, gross margin objectives, market prices, perceived value].

We review this pricing [monthly, quarterly, annually] to ensure that potential profits are not squandered. Customers seem willing to pay as much as [x] because of [explain reasoning].

Distribution Channels

The distribution channels we use for our product are [wholesalers, cataloguers, mass merchant retailers, consolidators]. These make sense for delivering our product to the end user because [customer profile, geography, seasonal swings]. The competition uses the [wholesalers, cataloguers, mass merchant retailers, consolidators] channel. Our channel will prove more advantageous because [x].

Our major current customers include; [list top five, with one or two sentence descriptions]. The attached chart [see appendix z] demonstrates how our product reaches the customer.

Advertising, Promotion, Trade Shows

Your purpose is to introduce, promote, and support your products in the marketplace. Although considered a cost, a properly designed and executed campaign is an investment.

[Your Company Name] has developed a comprehensive advertising and promotion strategy, which will be implemented by the best possible firm when funded is completed. We expect to have a presence in several national magazines as well as the trade press. We will produce our own ads and be a part of ad campaigns of our JV partners or OEMs. Our publicity plan is to remain in constant contact with editors and writers of the [trade journals that serve our industry] and seek stories and coverage that will [enhance our reputation, introduce us to buyers].

We plan to promote our product through a variety of [on site product sampling, demonstrations at high profile events, give-aways at fund raisers] and other high leverage events. The objective of all our promotions is to [expand the audience, position our product as a premium brand, strengthen our ties to the community].

[Your company name] participates in the following trade shows; [list trade shows, briefly describe organization that sponsors it and who attends, and describe presence there]. We have a regular [20 foot display booth of knock down construction which allows us to display our existing products and introduce new ones, or we prefer to attend trade shows as visitors and walk the show while displaying our wares only to pre-qualified buyers who will come to our nearby hospitality suite]. The following factors are taken into account when considering a trade show; will this event help deliver our message to our target audience? Does the location of the show have significance? Is the time frame convenient? Is it a "must-go show"?

COMPETITION

Tell us about key competitors in regard to product, price, location, promotion, management, and financial position. False or incomplete information here translates as dishonesty and negligence to investors, bankers, etc. Do not delude yourself (or your investors) about your competition.

Look in your telephone book's yellow pages. Look in the industrial directories at your local library. Search on-line databases that provide competitive profiles of other companies. Read industry magazines and look for advertisers.

We have no direct competition, but there are alternatives to our [product or service] in the marketplace.

or

We compete directly with [name competitor a, b, and c].

Provide a sample of each...[example...Acme Inc. is a $3 million sales manufacturer and marketer of pencils in the Northeast region. Acme Inc. is a division of Acme Corp, a public company with $800 million sales. The division sells pencils, pens, and other writing and drawing instruments. The recent trend for the division has been static, as the parent has not provided working capital to modernize machinery. Acme Inc. is managed by one Vice President who has been there for six months. The previous manager worked there for 11 months.]

The competition [does,doesn't] [use the same means of distribution as the company, advertise in the same trade journals]. *If the advertising is regular-it probably works!*

Our [product or service] is unique because of [x] and/or we have a competitive advantage because of our [speed to market, established brand name, low cost producer status].

RISK/OPPORTUNITY

Business Risks

This is also a critically important part of the plan. Knowing your risks and having a strategy is a must for attracting an investor. There are several kinds of risk, especially among entrepreneurial, growing businesses. Be sure to address the following, and provide your strategy for dealing with them.

Some of the major risks facing our development include [limited operating history; limited resources; market uncertainties; production uncertainties; limited management experience, dependence on key management].

Opportunities

This is also a critically important part of the plan. Use it to provide excitement and promise.

Although our business today has its share of risk, we feel we can overcome these risks because of [x]. We will address [market risk] by [doing a comprehensive study, partnering with a larger company who knows the market]. We feel we can address [pricing risk, product risk, management risk] by focusing on [x].

If we are able to overcome these risks, our company has the opportunity to [dominate a niche in the marketplace, become a major force in the industry]. We feel our brand could become know as the [place entrepreneurs look for financing help, the place people look for good tasting, low fat cheese]. We think we can achieve this goal in the next [x] years.

Specifically, our lead product [x], has the chance to [change the industry, affect many lives, improve performance in the [x] field]. This would also enable us to tap markets we have not yet begun to approach, such as [international sales, ethnic market, genX].

MANAGEMENT TEAM

It's cliche, but true: investing is a people business. Tell us not only about your managers, but how they work together as a team.

Our team has the following members to achieve our plan. [x] men and women who have a combined [x] years of experience; [y] years in marketing, [y] years in product development, and [y] years in [other disciplines].

Frankly, if you have more than a few people filling these positions, you're lucky. Tell us who you have, how much they have aged, and how much of the company they own.

Officers and Key Employees	Age	Stock
[A], President		
[B], Vice President of Marketing		
[C], Vice President of Sales		
[D], Vice President of Finance		
[E], Vice President of R & D		
[F], Vice President of Operations		
[G], Controller		
[H], Corporate Attorney		

Ownership

The company has authorized [x] shares of common stock, of which [100] are issued and outstanding. The following persons or organizations are significant owners of the company;

Name	# Shares Held	% Ownership
[A. B. Founder]	52	[52%]
[C. R. Inventor]	22	[22%]
Management Team	10	[10%]
[Seed Ventures]	10	[10%]

Professional Support

We have strung together a team of professionals, including:

[Corporate Attorney]

[Accounting Firm]

[Other Consultants]

Board of [Advisors, Directors]

We have also secured the assistance and support of the following business and industry experts to help in the decision making, strategizing, and opportunity pouncing process;

Highlight your board members, detailing where and why they add strategic importance, what experience they have and what contacts they can contribute.

CAPITAL REQUIREMENTS

Needless to say, this is important — state what your capital require-ments are.

We seek [$] of additional [equity, sub-debt, or senior financing] to fund our growth for the next [two years, year, month]. At that time, we will need an additional [$x] to reach a positive cash flow position.

The initial stage of funding will be used to [complete development, purchase equipment, introduce and market our new/next product line, fund working capital, acquire a competitor]. Here is a breakdown of how the funds will be spent;

complete development	[$x]
purchase equipment	[$x]
market our new/next product line	[$x]
fund working capital	[$x]

We can provide and exit for this [loan, investment] within [x] years by [a dividend of excess profits, recapitalizations, sale of company, or public offering].

Define how much time you will require to pay back the loan or provide a return to investors. And tell us how the repayment will be accomplished, and what strategy will be used to achieve that exit.

Conclusion

Be bold. This is the finale of the entire document.

Based on our projections, we feel an [investment in, loan to] our Company is a sound business investment. In order to proceed, we are requesting an [investment, loan] of $[x] by [date].

FINANCIAL PLAN

Needless to say, this is important — state what your capital requirements are.

Assumptions

The attached projections assume the following:

Income   Statements

We recommend that financial statements be monthly for the first year or two, then quarterly thereafter. Incorporate year to date figures if they exist.

Sales will increase with the introduction of the [new line, improved line]. We plan to introduce these products roughly on the following schedule: [detail here]. And we expect to be able to sell at the rate of [x] units per month within [x] months of introduction.

Cost of good sold will [decrease as a percentage] as we are able to buy more efficiently in the marketplace and use our new equipment to produce more units at lower cost.

Gross profit will remain static as [new introductions will be at higher margins, while we expect margins of older lines to erode].

Selling and administration expense will increase in absolute dollars, but decrease as a percentage because while expense is increasing, [name largest items here, or items that will change most significantly] our sales will be growing faster.

Research and Development, which will appear as a high percentage of sales early, will be reduced as a percentage over time.

Our head count will increase after funding to [x], which will include a [VP-Sales, paid on commission; VP R&D, $[x], VP Finance, $[x]; VP Operations, $[x].

Keep in mind that projections do not stand on their own. The rationale of how you prepared the numbers- and how sober you were when you did them- is important to investors. Expect to tie in the discussions you made about market size, time to market, market acceptance, and competitive pressures to tie into these numbers.

Discuss any large numbers or numbers that change significantly from period to period. Include discussion of sales growth rationale, expense growth, etc.

Balance Sheet Summary

Comment on any large or unusual items, such as other current assets, other accounts payable, or accrued liabilities.

Cash Flow and Break Even Analysis

These are critical statements, even more so than the Balance Sheets and Income Statements. Cash, and how much you have at the end of the day, is everything to investors.

We have assumed that our suppliers will be willing to grant us terms of [x] until we reach monthly purchases of [x]. At that time, we have assumed that our terms will be stretched to [x] days.

We have also assumed that we can collect our billings within [x] days because of [special programs with large customers, factoring arrangement, credit card and COD sales].

We have assumed that the first part of our [loan, investment] will be made in [month], and the balance in [month].

We can reach break even by the [x] month. Sales are expected to be at the [$x] level by that date.

EXHIBITS

A common error is mucking up the body of a plan with too much detail. That's what the exhibits are for.

Exhibits give an investor a better feel for the company behind the numbers. Be sure to include illustrative material such as:

- ▸ *Product literature and brochures*
- ▸ *Sales sheets*
- ▸ *Media coverage*
- ▸ *Clips from industry publications*
- ▸ *Relevant patents*
- ▸ *Market research data*
- ▸ *Past advertising campaigns*
- ▸ *Useful photographs of facilities, warehouses etc.*

Marketing Plan ▼ ▼ ▼

HOW TO DEVELOP A MARKETING PLAN

The marketing plan is a problem-solving document. Skilled problem solvers recognize that a big problem is usually the combination of several smaller problems. The best approach is to solve each of the smaller problems first, thereby dividing the big problem into manageable pieces. Your marketing plan should take the same approach. It should be a guide on which to base decisions and should ensure that everyone in your organization is working together to achieve the same goals. A good marketing plan can prevent your organization from reacting to problems in a piecemeal manner and even help in anticipating problems. Before your marketing plan can be developed, research must give you the basic guidelines: for whom you are designing your product or service (market segmentation), and exactly what that product or service should mean to those in the marketplace (market positioning). Below are some guidelines to help you develop a marketing plan to support the strategy you have selected for your organization.

MARKET SEGMENTATION

Your marketing plan should recognize the various segments of the market for your product or service and indicate how to adjust your product to reach those distinct markets. Instead of marketing a product in one way to everyone, you must recognize that some segments are not only different, but better than others for your product. This approach can be helpful in penetrating markets that would be too broad and undefined without segmentation. No matter what you are making or selling, take the total market and divide it up like a pie chart. The divisions can be based on various criteria such as those listed below.

Demographics

This is the study of the distribution, density and vital statistics of a population, and includes such characteristics as

> Sex
> Age
> Education
> Geographic location
> Home ownership versus rental
> Marital status
> Size of family unit
> Total income of family unit
> Ethnic or religious background
> Job classification blue collar versus salaried or professional

Psychographics

This is the study of how the human characteristics of consumers may have a bearing on their response to products, packaging, advertising and public relations efforts. Behavior may be measured as it involves an interplay among these broad sets of variables:

Predisposition - What is there about a person's past culture, heredity or upbringing that may influence his or her ability to consider purchasing one new product or service versus another?

Influences - What are the roles of social forces such as education, peer pressure or group acceptance in dictating a person's consumption patterns?

Product Attributes - What the product is or can be made to represent in the minds of consumers has a significant bearing on whether certain segments will accept the concept. These attributes may be suggested by the marketer or perceived by the customer. Some typical ways of describing a product include:

> **Price/value perception** - Is the item worth the price being asked?
>
> **Taste** - Does it have the right amount of sweetness or lightness?
>
> **Texture** - Does it have the accepted consistency or feel?
>
> **Quality** - What can be said about the quality of the ingredients or lack of artificial ingredients?
>
> **Benefits** - How does the consumer feel after using the product?

Trust - Can the consumer rely on this particular brand? What about the reputation of the manufacturer in standing behind the product?

Life-Style

Statements consumers make about themselves through conspicuous consumption can be put to good use by research people who read the signals correctly. By studying behavioral variables, such as a person's use of time, services and products, researchers can identify some common factors that can predict future behavior.

MARKET POSITIONING

You must realize that your product or service cannot be all things to all people. Very few items on the market today have universal appeal. Even when dealing in basic commodities like table salt or aspirin, marketing people have gone to all sorts of extremes to create brand awareness and product differentiation. If your product or service is properly positioned, prospective purchasers or users should immediately recognize its unique benefits or advantages and be better able to assess it in comparison to your competition's offering. Positioning is how you give your product or service brand identification.

Positioning involves analyzing each market segment as defined by your research activities and developing a distinct position for each segment. Ask yourself how you want to appear to that segment, or what you must do for that segment to ensure that it buys your product or service. This will dictate different media and advertising appeals for each segment. For example, you may sell the same product in a range of packages or sizes, or make cosmetic changes in the product, producing private labels or selecting separate distribution channels to reach the various segments. Beer, for example, is sold on tap and in seven-ounce bottles, twelve-ounce cans and bottles, six-packs, twelve-packs, cases, and quart bottles and kegs of several sizes. The beer is the same but each package size may appeal to a separate market segment and have to be sold with a totally different appeal and through different retail outlets.

Remember that your marketing position can, and should, change to meet the current conditions of the market for your product. The ability of your company to adjust will be enhanced greatly by an up-to-date knowledge of the marketplace gained through continual monitoring. By having good data about your customers, the segments they fit into and the buying motives of those segments, you can select the position that makes the most sense.

While there are many possible marketing positions, most would fit into one of the following categories:

> **Positioning on specific product features** - A very common approach, especially for industrial products. If your product or service has some unique features that have obvious value this may be the way to go.

> **Positioning on benefits** - Strongly related to positioning on product features. Generally, this is more effective because you can talk to your customers about what your product or service can do for them. The features may be nice, but

unless customers can be made to understand why the product will benefit them, you may not get the sale.

Positioning for a specific use - Related to benefit positioning. Consider Campbell's positioning of soups for cooking. An interesting extension is mood positioning: "Have a Coke and a smile." This works best when you can teach your customers how to use your product or when you use a promotional medium that allows a demonstration.

Positioning for user category - A few examples: "You've Come a Long Way Baby," "The Pepsi Generation" and "Breakfast of Champions." Be sure you show your product being used by models with whom your customers can identify.

Positioning against another product or a competing business - A strategy that ranges from implicit to explicit comparison. Implicit comparisons can be quite pointed; for example, Avis never mentions Hertz, but the message is clear. Explicit comparisons can take two major forms. The first form makes a comparison with a direct competitor and is aimed at attracting customers from the compared brand, which is usually the category leader. The second type does not attempt to attract the customers of the compared product, but rather uses the comparison as a reference point. Consider, for example, the positioning of the Volkswagen Dasher, which picks up speed faster than a Mercedes and has a bigger trunk than a Rolls Royce. This usually works to the advantage of the smaller business if you can capitalize on the tradition of cheering for the underdog. You can gain stature by comparing yourself to a larger competitor just as long as your customers remain convinced that you are trying harder.

Product class disassociation - A less common type of positioning. It is particularly effective when used to introduce a new product that differs from traditional products. Lead-free gasoline and tubeless tires were new product classes positioned against older products. Space-age technology may help you here. People have become accustomed to change and new products and are more willing to experiment than was true ten years ago. Even so, some people are more adventuresome and trusting than others and more apt to try a revolutionary product. The trick is to find out who are the potential brand switchers or experimenters and find out what it would take to get them to try your product. The obvious disadvantage of dealing with those who try new products is that they may move on to another brand just as easily. Brand loyalty is great as long as it is to your brand.

Hybrid bases - Incorporates elements from several types of positioning. Given the variety of possible bases for position-ing, small business owners should consider the possibility of a hybrid approach. This is particularly true in smaller towns where there aren't enough customers in any segment to justify the expense of separate marketing approaches.

MARKETING PLAN WORKSHEET

This is the marketing plan of

_____

Market Analysis

A. Target Market - Who are the customers?

1. We will be selling primarily to (check all that apply):
Percent of Business

     a. Private sector _____

     b. Wholesalers   _____

     c. Retailers   _____

     d. Government   _____

     e. Other   _____

2. We will be targeting customers by:

     a. Product line/services. We will target specific lines:

     _____

     b. Geographic area? Which areas?

     _____

     c. Sales? We will target sales of:

     _____

d. Industry? Our target industry is

_____

e. Other?

_____

3. How much will our selected market spend on our type of
product or service this coming year?

_____

B. Competition

1. Who are our competitors?

Name _____
Address _____
Years in Business _____
Market Share _____
Price/Strategy _____
Product/Service _____
Features _____

Name _____
Address _____
Years in Business _____
Market Share _____
Price/Strategy _____
Product/Service _____
Features _____

2. How competitive is the market?
      High   _____
      Medium _____
      Low   _____

3. List below your strengths and weaknesses compared to your competition (consider such areas as location, size of resources, reputation, services, personnel, etc.):

Strengths	Weaknesses
1._____	1._____
2._____	2._____
3._____	3._____
4._____	4._____

C. Environment

1. The following are some important economic factors that will affect our product or service (such as country growth, industry health, economic trends, taxes, rising energy prices, etc.):

_____
_____
_____

2. The following are some important legal factors that will affect our market:

_____
_____
_____

3. The following are some important government factors:

_____

_____

_____

4. The following are other environmental factors that will affect our market, but over which we have no control:

_____

_____

_____

Product or Service Analysis

A. Description

1. Describe here what the product/service is and what it does:

_____

_____

_____

B. Comparison

1. What advantages does our product/service have over those of the competition (consider such things as unique features, patents, expertise, special training, etc.)?

_____

_____

_____

_____

2. What disadvantages does it have?

_____

_____

_____

C. Some Considerations

1. Where will you get your materials and supplies?

_____

_____

_____

2. List other considerations:

_____

_____

_____

Marketing Strategies - Market Mix

A. Image

1. First, what kind of image do we want to have (such as cheap but good, or exclusiveness, or customer-oriented or highest quality, or convenience, or speed, or ...)?

_____

_____

_____

_____

B. Features

1. List the features we will emphasize:

    a. _____

    b. _____

    c. _____

C. Pricing

1. We will be using the following pricing strategy:

    a. Markup on cost _____ What % Markup? _____

    b. Suggested price _____

    c. Competitive _____

    d. Below competition _____

    e. Premium price _____

    f. Other _____

2. Are our prices in line with our image?

    YES ___ NO ___

3. Do our prices cover costs and leave a margin of profit?

    YES ___ NO ___

D. Customer Services

1. List the customer services we provide:

    a. _____

    b. _____

    c. _____

2. These are our sales/credit terms:

a. _____

b. _____

c. _____

3. The competition offers the following services:

a. _____

b. _____

c. _____

E. Advertising/Promotion

1. These are the things we wish to say about the business:

_____

_____

_____

2. We will use the following advertising/promotion sources:

a. Television _____

b. Radio _____

c. Direct mail _____

d. Personal contacts _____

e. Trade associations _____

f. Newspaper _____

g. Magazines _____

h. Yellow Pages _____

i. Billboard _____

j. Other _____

3. The following are the reasons why we consider the media we have chosen to be the most effective:

_____

_____

_____